"Linda brilliantly and biblically shines the light on exchanging the promised gift of peace for the crippling and unwanted stresses of life. Packed with [obscured by barcode], this book will free ´you to [obscured] peace."

—Ly[obscured] [obscured] *Times* bestselling author, *Unglued*; president, Proverbs 31 Ministries

Praise for *When You Don't Know What to Pray*

"The book's strength is Shepherd's heart for prayer and tenderness for her readers. Recommend to people who are struggling through difficult circumstances and to pastors and group leaders."

—**CBA Retailers + Resources**

"Linda has used powerful prayer to overcome the worst of circumstances, and you can too. She does not share pat answers, she shares truth that will transform your life. Are you ready to learn her prayer secrets? Bow your head and pray your way through this book."

—**LeAnn Thieman**, coauthor, *Chicken Soup for the Christian Woman's Soul* and *Chicken Soup for the Christian Soul 2*

"This book is a must-read for anyone who desires a stronger prayer life. Linda speaks from experience, and her stories compel the reader to pray more."

—**Carole Lewis**, national director, First Place, www.firstplace.org

"Linda Evans Shepherd is a woman of prayer, and in a world of crisis, change, and constant challenges, what woman doesn't need to learn more about the praying life? Pick up this book to gain an encouraged and equipped heart."

—**Pam Farrel**, international speaker;
relationship specialist; author, *Men Are Like Waffles,
Women Are Like Spaghetti*

Praise for *Experiencing God's Presence*

"If you long for a relationship with God that is deeper, richer, and more intimate than you've ever known before, read this book. In *Experiencing God's Presence*, Linda Evans Shepherd reveals the secrets of learning how to listen to God during your prayer times. Each chapter is filled with practical, biblical tools that will enrich your prayer life and draw you closer to the heart of the Father."

—**Carol Kent**, speaker; author,
When I Lay My Isaac Down

"*Experiencing God's Presence* will transform your prayer life! Please buy this book."

—**Elaine Miller**, author, *Splashes of Serenity*

HOW TO
PRAY
IN TIMES OF
STRESS

HOW TO
PRAY
IN TIMES OF
STRESS

Linda Evans Shepherd

SPIRE

Published by Revell
a division of Baker Publishing Group
P.O. Box 6287, Grand Rapids, MI 49516-6287
www.revellbooks.com

Spire edition published 2018
ISBN 978-0-8007-2908-0

Previously published under the title *The Stress Cure*

Printed in the United States of America

In memory of my dad—
James Leroy Evans.
A godly man, a wonderful husband, and a dear father.
No daughter had a better daddy.

Contents

Acknowledgments

Thank you, dear family, for your love and support as I wrote this book. I want to thank my dear husband and my son, as you are always there for me. I'm also sending a special thank-you to my daughter—Miss Laura—who stays joyful no matter her challenges. You are an inspiration.

I'm also sending a shout out to my wonderful praying friends in the Advanced Writers and Speakers Association (AWSA) and my precious prayer partner, Carole. Also, a special thank-you to Team Shepherd for all you do. I so appreciate you all.

Also, a special thanks to my editor, Vicki Crumpton, and my agent, Janet Kobobel Grant, as well as all my wonderful friends at Baker Publishing Group. It has been such a blessing to partner with you in publishing this much needed message.

And finally, thank you, dear readers, for opening this book. The thing I most loved about writing it is that it helped me go deeper into the mysteries of God's joy, peace, and presence. My prayer is that this book will do the same for you.

I love you all very much!

Introduction

The Problem of Stress

Peace be with you.

Luke 24:36

A clock would make a poor bank. No customer would ever be able to deposit a moment to save for later because, at the end of the day, every second would be spent and the clock would be bankrupt.

While it's true that each day gives us twenty-four hours to spend, those hours have to be divided into moments driven by the demands of our to-do lists, not to mention our problems, worries, families, and jobs. It seems that our minutes evaporate no matter how fast we rush to meet them. The ticking of the clock is one of the reasons why, according to *Psychology Today*, 39 percent of Americans claimed their stress had increased over the past year. The article continues with unsettling news: "More alarming, only 29 percent reported that they were doing an 'excellent' or 'very good' job at managing their stress."[1]

We'll get up tomorrow with a brand-new set of twenty-four hours, a new day that will give us another chance to catch up, find solutions to our challenges, and—hopefully—calm down. Yet, by the end of tomorrow, many of us will fail to find solutions to our stressors. A recent survey shows that most people hear alarm bells when it comes to money (75%), work (70%), the economy (67%), relationships (58%), family responsibilities (57%), family's health (53%), personal health (53%), job stability (49%), housing (49%), and personal safety (32%).[2]

If we can't find a way to quiet these alarms, we could be in for even more stress, which eventually impacts our health. Web MD explains:

> If stress happens too often or lasts too long, it can have bad effects. It can be linked to headaches, an upset stomach, back pain, and trouble sleeping. It can weaken your immune system, making it harder to fight off disease. If you already have a health problem, stress may make it worse. It can make you moody, tense, or depressed. Your relationships may suffer, and you may not do well at work or school.[3]

Not only that, but stress contributes to conditions such as fatigue, poor concentration, irritability, a quick temper, obesity, cancer, stroke, heart attack, and even death.

Yikes! The thought of the effects of stress is enough to stress out anyone.

Before I start to tell you the secrets to taming stress, let's define it. Wikipedia defines stress as "a negative concept that can have an impact on one's mental and physical well-being,"[4] while the World English Dictionary describes it as "mental, emotional, or physical strain or tension."[5]

Besides the mental and physical impacts of stress, stress can also impact our spiritual well-being with what I call "soul blocks." These include such things as harboring offenses, the feeling of being overwhelmed or out of control, continually striving for more, frustrations, burdens, hopelessness, offenses, anxiety, bad attitudes, distractions, and depression.

But I have good news! I've felt the effects of these negative consequences more than a few times, and I've discovered powerful solutions that can help you build bridges over your stressors so you can journey on to peace, as well as to "love, joy, . . . forbearance, kindness, goodness, faithfulness, gentleness and self-control" (Gal. 5:22–23).

Though it's true that we all get twenty-four hours each day, we can choose to spend our time filled with anxiety, or we can push toward God's peace that passes understanding. Building a bridge to peace involves gaining a better understanding of God and the tools he's given us, which include prayer and God's Word.

As for me? I would love to tell you that I've eliminated all stress from my life, but as a fellow traveler who happens to be married with kids, I often get opportunities to test God's solutions of peace in my own crazy life, which includes a profoundly disabled daughter, the recent death of my father, and book deadlines. So, yes, I know the taste and feel of stress. Yet, I've also tasted and felt God's peace. I've learned to use the tools of prayer and God's Word, tools we will use together throughout the pages of this book.

A Stressful Day

Not long ago, I heard a radio preacher say, "If you have stress, that means you're not trusting God." I was having a stressful day, so I didn't particularly care for this remark. I silently argued, *Why of course I trust God. My problem is I'm having a day that won't let me "phone it in."*

My stressful day started the morning I had to drive fifty miles to get to a live radio interview in another town. As the clock ticked down to the time I had to leave, everything started to go wrong. I suddenly remembered I needed to get a tax report in the mail, and then my college son called to tell me the registration tags on his car had expired six months ago. He needed me to run down to the county clerk with my checkbook in hand, as he lived out of town and couldn't take care of this errand himself.

While racing to finish the tax report, I made a call to the county clerk to see if I could pay the car fee by phone. "You can't phone it in because it will take a month for your son to get the new registration sticker," the clerk admonished. "His car could be impounded by then. Come in today and, if possible, bring cash."

As I felt my stress level rise, I got another call telling me my office payroll was late, a payroll I had to sign before I left town so my assistant could buy groceries, a habit she didn't like to break. By the time I finished the tax report, signed the payroll, and paid the car fee, my stress was running high, as I was now running late for the radio interview, an interview I could not phone in.

So I hopped in my car and, with sweat trickling between my shoulder blades, raced through freeway traffic for fifty miles. When I arrived, I had to park a block away before sprinting to the building to catch the elevator. When the elevator opened at the top floor, I dashed down the hall and slipped into the chair and headphones as the radio station's mike went live. The host barely managed to whisper, "I was beginning to think you wouldn't make it!"

By the time I got back home, I was exhausted. The next morning, instead of feeling relieved that the stress was over, I found myself reliving it. That's when a friend called and asked, "You sound stressed. What's wrong?"

Happily, I rattled off my list of yesterday's woes, a list I was sure would cause Sara to gush, "Oh, Linda! I can hardly imagine."

Instead, Sara replied, "Is that all? I have four of my five kids on the couch with the stomach flu, each with their own bucket!"

"Oh, Sara!" I cried. "Your stress trumps mine!"

We shared a laugh, but after we hung up, I wondered why I'd allowed yesterday's stress to block God's peace, peace I could have had today. I hated to admit it, but that radio preacher had been right in part. Though we can't control all the things that happen to us, we can, with God's help, control our reaction to them—trusting God even when we're stressed.

The Story of Peace

Throughout this book, I'm going to share stories based on God's Word and told through my imagination. For example, when I think of the disciples, frightened and hiding after the crucifixion of Jesus, this is how I imagine the scene.

The disciples sat in the upper room with the window shuttered against the bustle of a bright Jerusalem day. They sat quietly, hardly daring to move lest their footfalls or voices be overheard by a passerby. Even so, they occasionally muttered things like, "And we thought he was the Messiah."

One of the shadows belonged to Mark. He shifted a bit and said, "But did you hear that the women reported his tomb was empty and . . ."

Another shadow wrung his hands. "That's just proof that they're mad with grief."

Peter, from a darkened corner, added, "And fear. I saw the tomb myself, and it was empty, the body probably moved."

"Quiet. I hear the sound of soldiers in the street," Andrew whispered.

Luke rose. "Have they found us so soon?" He peeked through a crack in the wooden slats, then announced with relief, "They've passed us by."

"For now," Peter said. "Perhaps we should have gone to Emmaus with Cleopas and his cousin, at least until things cool off."

"But what about the women's report?" Mark asked. "Mary seemed to believe. What if Jesus did rise from the dead?"

A soft knock sounded at the door. No one spoke, until a muffled voice called out, "It's me, Cleopas, and my cousin. We have news."

Peter sprang to his feet and unbolted the door to let the men slip into the room. He asked, "Then we're to be arrested?"

Cleopas announced, "We've seen . . ."

Peter fingered the sheath strapped to his belt. "The soldiers are on their way?"

"The Lord!" cousin Ethan blurted. "We've seen the Lord!"

Cleopas explained, "Earlier tonight Jesus walked home with us and . . ."

"Our hearts burned within us as he explained the Scriptures, about why he had to die and . . ."

"We didn't recognize him until . . ."

"Until he broke bread with us. That's when we saw his wounded hands and . . ."

Suddenly, a brilliant glow filled the room and Jesus appeared. He held out his nail-pierced hands and spoke his first words to his disciples since his death. "Peace be with you."

The men, minus Thomas, who'd slipped away to buy bread, stood stunned, doubting their very eyes until Jesus showed them the wound in his side. The men were soon filled with joy, for they understood. Jesus had walked through the wall of death and into life, just as he had walked through the walls of their doubt to bring them peace (based on Luke 24:13–39).

Not only did Jesus walk through the wall of the upper room, but he can also walk through your walls of doubt, fear, and stress and bring you peace. But first you have to invite him into your life. You can start with a prayer like this:

Dear Jesus,

I need you to walk through the walls of my doubt and unbelief. I choose to believe you are alive! Give me supernatural belief so that I can see you more clearly. You died on the cross for my sins and came back to life again. Because you took my punishment, I can now walk with God.

I turn from my sins and turn to you, to follow you and to trust you with my whole heart. Please forgive me for my past and let your Spirit come inside me so I can learn how to walk in your peace.

In Jesus's name, amen.

It's good that you prayed this prayer, for although Jesus can walk through walls, he's a gentleman and never goes where he's not invited.

Shalom, my friend. Throughout the pages of this book, I will help you unpack the prayer tools of peace Christ has given to us. But for now know that his words to his disciples are also his words for you: "Peace be with you."

You'll see. Everything is going to be all right.

1

The Key to Peace

Finding More of God's Presence

> The mystery in a nutshell is just this: Christ is
> in you, so therefore you can look forward to
> sharing in God's glory. It's that simple.
>
> Colossians 1:27 Message

My Introduction to the Prince of Peace

When I was nine years old, a group of girls from my church
and I piled into my mother's car and went to our church
camp nestled beside a cow pasture near Newton, Texas. In
between splashing in the swimming pool in the sweltering
heat, singing campfire songs under the balmy stars, and hanging our tempera-painted crafts from a clothesline, we listened
to the speaker for the week nightly implore us to come to
faith. After his message, the young pastor would extend an

invitation to all those who wanted "Jesus in their hearts" to come forward. I would stand with my row and sing the old hymn "I Surrender All," watching repentant girls make their way to the front of the meeting. As we sang, I also watched my mother, who stood with her head bowed as she fervently prayed for my soul.

One morning, the older girls in our group cornered me outside the dining hall. "Linda, your mother told us that you aren't saved. We want you to know we're praying for you."

My cheeks burned. "My mother told you that?"

Donna, the oldest girl at about thirteen, said, "Don't be mad. It's just that your mom is very worried about you and asked us to pray." The girls tried to blink back tears. "Linda, won't you please come to faith in Jesus at the meeting tonight?" they pleaded.

"I've been thinking about it," I admitted. "But tomorrow night is our last night at camp, and with tomorrow being my birthday, I'm thinking of waiting until then."

Before the girls could hug me, I warned them, "But you can't tell my mother. If you tell, I won't go down for the altar call, and that's a promise."

Their heads bobbed. "Don't worry, Linda, we won't tell."

I felt relieved. I so wanted to go forward, but this had to be my decision, not my mom's. I breathed a sigh of relief and skipped off to arts and crafts, knowing that if these girls kept their word, I would soon know Jesus as my Lord and Savior.

But the next evening, just before the start of the service, my mother hugged me and gushed, "Linda, the girls told me you are coming to faith tonight. I'm so proud."

My heart stopped. "But the girls promised they wouldn't tell."

"Honey, they just wanted me to know, and I'm so glad."

I felt like crying as I tried to explain, "This is something I need to do by myself. Now I won't be able to go forward tonight."

I hated the hurt look on my mother's face, but I couldn't help it. This was a decision I wanted to make myself, without her influence. So during the altar call that night, as two hundred girls sang "I Surrender All," I crossed my little arms and set my jaw and didn't surrender a thing. If the girls wouldn't keep our agreement, neither would I. Despite the quiet weeping of Donna and her friends, and even though I desperately wanted to bolt to the front of the camp meeting to get Jesus into my heart, I stood my ground. A promise was a promise.

The next morning, I began to realize the impact of my obstinacy as the older girls shot me looks of disappointment as we packed our suitcases for home. Though they had nothing to say to me, their swollen eyes and sad expressions spoke for them. How could you refuse Jesus? How could you hurt your mother like this? That's when it began to dawn on me. What a bad little girl I must be!

The disappointment of the older girls was nothing compared to my mom's. As we drove home in silence, I felt my mom's profound sadness hover over the car. Now, for the first time in my life, I felt the weight of my sin.

I continued to feel this weight, especially during the altar calls at my church every Sunday morning, Sunday evening, and Wednesday night for the next several months. I longed to go forward but couldn't bear the thought of surrendering to my mother before I surrendered to Christ.

Still, I worried what would happen if I was killed in a car crash and went to hell. Our pastor had described hell as such a frightening place. I knew I didn't want to spend eternity burning in the flames of God's wrath. Plus, I was worried about what my pastor called the rapture, the day Jesus would come back to earth with a shout and take all the believers to heaven, leaving only those of us who had refused to come to faith to face the terrible plagues at the end of times. That's why, whenever the house got too quiet, I would rush to check on my family to see if Jesus had somehow taken them and left me behind.

It wasn't until early November, when my church held an evening Vacation Bible School, that I finally saw my opportunity. That first night of VBS class, my fifth-grade teacher passed out printed note cards and stubby pencils. The cards asked if we wanted Jesus to come into our hearts; check yes or no.

Without the prying eyes of my mother, I was more than relieved to check yes.

The next question asked if we would like to talk to the pastor. I checked yes again, never dreaming that the pastor would soon be on the phone with my mother to arrange a home visit.

So the following afternoon after school, with my mother hovering in the kitchen listening in on the conversation between me, our pastor, and the visiting evangelist, I prayed the famous sinner's prayer. "Dear Lord, I repent of my sins. Please forgive me. I invite Jesus to come into my heart, to be Lord of my life. In Jesus's name, amen."

After I said the prayer, the men looked at me expectantly, but I felt disappointed. This was the same old prayer I'd silently prayed almost every Sunday and Wednesday since I was six. I'd expected to feel relief and joy, yet I felt nothing but embarrassment at the overwhelming joy of my mother.

But later that night at church, after my VBS class and during Evangelist Bob's sermon, I was surprised when he told the church congregation, "Just this afternoon I saw a young junior girl come to faith."

My heart skipped a beat. He was talking about me! And the thing that so impressed me was that Evangelist Bob had *seen* me come to faith despite the fact that I hadn't felt anything when I'd prayed. That's when I knew it must be real! Jesus was in my heart at last.

At the end of the service, the moment I'd dreaded came. It was finally time to do the one thing I'd so far failed to do, to surrender everything—including my stubborn will—and to give the Lord the lordship of my life. Evangelist Bob extended the invitation for all those who had made decisions to follow Christ to come forward as we sang, you guessed it, "I Surrender All."

This time I didn't have a choice, and though my mother was watching, I pushed through the row of kids from my class to the aisle, where I finally made my way to the front of the auditorium to surrender everything and to make my profession of faith public for the first time. But something unexpected occurred. As I walked to the front of the auditorium, my wall of stubbornness burst and the Holy Spirit rushed into my soul. I was so overwhelmed that despite my embarrassment I broke down into sobs that wouldn't stop, not even after the hymn ended—and not even after the people of the church had all shaken my hand to congratulate me for joining the family of God.

I've long thought about that moment, when in a flood of tears that final wall of pride that had held me back from the full presence of God fell away. I believe God's Holy Spirit touched my soul as I became a new creation in Christ, an actual dwelling place for the Lord's presence.

The Temple of God's Presence

Does God really enter into our spirits like that? Yes. The second chapter of Ephesians says, "Together, we are his house, built on the foundation of the apostles and the prophets. And the cornerstone is Christ Jesus himself. We are carefully joined together in him, becoming a holy temple for the Lord. Through him you Gentiles are also being made part of this dwelling where God lives by his Spirit" (vv. 20–22 TLB).

I believe I was "saved," "born again," or "pardoned for my sin by God" perhaps even the first time I secretly called upon the name of Jesus when I was only six. However, I also believe that the moment I was able to push past my pride and go public with my decision, the final wall came down, and I was transformed from a stubborn ten-year-old to a person filled with the Holy Spirit. Today, decades later, the Holy Spirit still resides within me, and I am indeed a new creation in Christ, as 2 Corinthians 5:17 explains: "Therefore, if anyone is in Christ, the new creation has come: The old is gone, the new is here!" The Living Bible reads, "When someone becomes a Christian, he becomes a brand new person inside. He is not the same anymore. A new life has begun!"

Did you know that until Christ's resurrection from the dead humanity endured a great rift with God that started back in the Garden of Eden? The garden's inhabitants, Adam and Eve, once had such access to God that they walked with him unashamed, clothed only in their innocence.

The rift between God and this man and woman started when this couple broke God's only rule: not to eat the fruit from the tree in the middle of the garden. Not realizing the fruit would poison them with sin, the two bit into trouble. It was in that moment that Adam's and Eve's eyes were opened and they saw that they were naked. In their shame, they did something they'd never done before. They hid from God.

Humankind has been hiding from God ever since, unworthy to be in the presence of such an awesome, holy being. To help remedy this rift, God's people turned their stone altars red with the blood of bulls and goats as they followed God's directive to cover their sins with the blood of their sacrifices. Still, their efforts to hide their sins from God dissolved each time they failed to follow each of God's laws to the letter. Their constant failure kept the people slaves to a law they couldn't keep. It wasn't until Jesus's death on the cross that the rift between God and humankind was finally bridged. Now, through Jesus's sacrifice, his blood covers our sins, breaking us free from the law of sin and death.

God's very presence has become available not only to clothe us in the righteousness of Jesus but also to enter into our very beings. In fact, when we call out to Jesus, his righteousness descends on us like a garment, and his Holy Spirit dwells within us, transforming us from the inside out.

But just who is this Holy Spirit? Jesus described him in John 14:17 when he said, "He is the Spirit, who reveals the truth about God. The world cannot receive him, because it cannot see him or know him. But you know him, because he remains with you and is in you" (GNT).

Jesus introduced the Holy Spirit to his disciples this way: "But I am telling you the truth: it is better for you that I go away, because if I do not go, the Helper will not come to you. But if I do go away, then I will send him to you" (John 16:7 GNT).

Max Lucado explains:

> If I were to ask you to tell me what Jesus did for you, you'd likely give a cogent answer. But if I were to ask you the role of the Holy Spirit in your life . . . ? Eyes would duck. Throats would be cleared. And it would be obvious that of the three persons of the Godhead, the Holy Spirit is the one we understand the least. Perhaps the most common mistake made regarding the Holy Spirit is perceiving him as a power and not a person, a force with no identity. Such is not true. The Holy Spirit is a person.[1]

As Lucado reminds us, the person of the Holy Spirit helps us (John 16:7), he convicts the lost to turn to God (John 16:8), and he leads us in all truth (John 16:13). It is the Spirit who helps us tear down our walls, makes miracles of our messes, comforts our heartaches, and leads us to breakthroughs. Lucado believes that God's Holy Spirit is already at work in our lives. He says, "By the way, for those of us who spent years trying to do God's job that is great news. It's much easier to raise the sail than row the boat."[2]

This *is* great news, because we have the Helper, the Counselor, living inside us. All we have to do is let the breath of God fill our sails to power us through our stressors and into the peace of God.

I have spent so much time explaining the Holy Spirit in this chapter because we will be using his tools to help us tear down the fear, stress, worry, and heartbreak that have walled us from the peace that Jesus came to give us. Jesus explained in John 14:27, "Peace I leave with you, My peace I give to you; not as the world gives do I give to you. Let not your heart be troubled, neither let it be afraid" (NKJV).

It's in fact the Holy Spirit who can give us the supernatural peace of Christ that will help us de-stress. But what must we do in order to enjoy this peace?

To get our first clue, let's go back in time to the day the Comforter arrived. Here's how I picture the scene.

The Story of Peace Continued

Peter looked around the table at the surviving apostles, plus Matthias, serving as Judas's replacement. Peter cleared his throat. "My friends, do you realize it's been fifty days since we broke bread here with Jesus at Passover?"

Thomas walked to the window of the upper room and looked down at the street through the slats of the tightly closed shutters. He turned to face his brothers. "It's so hard to believe it's already Pentecost. But the streets never lie; they are teeming with people who've come from near and far to celebrate the holiday."

"What I want to know," Andrew said, "is how much longer we are to wait here."

Peter responded, "What does it matter? If Jesus told us to wait, we wait!"

Thomas interrupted, "Agreed, of course. But what exactly are we waiting for?"

Matthew looked up from writing on a scroll and reminded the group, "Jesus said not to leave Jerusalem until his Father baptized us with the Holy Spirit."

Thomas shook his head and strode back to the table. "I don't get it. When a man has been baptized in the Jordon River, he can wring water from his beard, but how will a man know when he's been baptized by this Holy Spirit?"

The silence that hung in the air shattered as the shutters slammed open with a great blast of wind that whirled through the room, extinguishing the candles on the table.

As the candlewicks trailed smoke, the men gasped as a flame appeared over each of their heads, as if they were *human* candles on fire with the Spirit of God.

Thomas was the first to speak. His voice lifted in the babbling tongue of a Mede, a language that he, a man of Galilee, had never learned. Thomas's voice was soon joined by that of John, who was speaking fluidly in a tongue of Egypt. The babbling grew as one by one the disciples began to speak in a language they had never known before.

As God's Spirit joined with their spirits, they were emboldened and rushed down the stairs and into the street, each calling out in the language they'd been given. In moments, clusters of passersby surrounded every disciple, shouting questions in the same tongues in which the disciples proclaimed.

The roar of voices soon generated a mob. The voice of a man could be heard yelling, "They're drunk!" and many heads nodded as if to say, "What else could it be?"

In answer, Peter climbed up on a nearby cart, then motioned for the crowd to be silent. He spoke to them in clear Aramaic. "These men are not drunk. It's only 9 a.m. after all."

The crowd blinked back surprise at the discovery that Peter's words were not slurred with wine. A tall Roman merchant shouted out, "Then what's happening here? I can see that these men are locals, nothing but uneducated fishermen.

Who taught them to speak in our own tongues about the things God has done?"

Peter's face glowed as he exclaimed, "It's happened as the prophet Joel predicted. God is pouring out his Spirit on all people—men and women alike. Our sons and daughters will prophesy, young men will see visions, and old men will dream dreams. The heavens will show signs and wonders, as will the earth with signs of blood and fire, clouds of smoke, and the sightings of a red moon, all before Jesus returns. But those who call upon the name of the Lord will be saved."

"What does it all mean?" a man with a Judean accent shouted.

"Don't you see?" Peter replied. "It's all about Jesus, the Holy One who lived among us, who was endorsed by God to do signs and wonders, as you well know. He was the one who died in the horror of the cross—the Holy One who, as King David predicted, would not rot in the grave but would instead make his enemies his footstool."

"Are we then his enemies?" a dark-skinned Libyan called to Peter.

"God has raised Jesus from the dead, and we are his witnesses. But do you not understand?" Peter motioned to the crowd. "You have crucified our Lord the Messiah!"

A Jewish farmer cried out, "What should we do?"

Peter answered, "You must each repent of your sins, turn to God, and be baptized in the name of Jesus Christ for the forgiveness of your sins. Then you too will receive the gift of the Holy Spirit."

The crowd responded to Peter's call, and that day three thousand men were baptized by the disciples in both water and the Holy Spirit (based on Acts 1–2).

Shine the Light of the Word

Just as those Galilean disciples were ignited with the flame of the Holy Spirit, we too should be filled with the Holy Spirit. It's like Billy Graham explained:

> The first truth we must understand is that God has given us his Holy Spirit, and that he dwells within us. If I have accepted Christ as my Savior, the Spirit of God dwells within me. Remember—I might not necessarily *feel* his presence, but that does not mean he is absent. It is the *fact* of his presence we must understand. God has promised that his Spirit lives with you if you belong to Christ, and God cannot lie. *We must accept this fact by faith.*[3]

I agree with Graham that when we come to faith the flame of the Spirit of God mingles with our souls, making us new creations filled with the very presence of God himself. But having his Spirit inside us doesn't necessarily mean we know how to yield to him. And this yielding could very well be the key to experiencing less stress in our lives.

Before we pray a yielding prayer, let's look at what Paul says about the Holy Spirit in Galatians 5:25: "Since we are living by the Spirit, let us follow the Spirit's leading in every part of our lives" (NLT). Note that this verse indicates that we *can* live by the Spirit, meaning that it is possible to tap into the power of God, not to control God but to be controlled by God.

Pray, "Lord, open my eyes to see your truth as I read Galatians 5:25 again."

Let's yield to the presence of the Holy Spirit through prayer.

Yielding Prayer

Dear Lord,

How glad I am that you've redeemed me for yourself. Thank you! Thank you also that when I came to faith your Holy Spirit touched my very soul to indwell me. I am now a new creation in Christ, your temple filled with your presence. Lord, I invite more of your presence. Teach me how to yield to your Spirit so I can follow your leading in every area of my life—including my stress. Teach me the secret of having more peace in, through, and despite my circumstances.

In Jesus's name, amen.

2

Overwhelmed

Finding Relief When the World Closes In

And let the peace that comes from Christ rule
in your hearts.

Colossians 3:15 NLT

Have you ever seen an episode of the A&E TV show *Hoarders*? It's a show about perfectly normal-looking people who live in perfectly normal-looking houses who become overwhelmed by their possessions. Their problems start when what appears to be an innocent collection of baseball cards takes over the attic. Meanwhile, a pile of magazines stashed in a closet forces its way into the hallway before claiming the living room. But that's nothing compared to the sacks of bargains—beautiful new clothes with the price tags attached, shiny red blenders, and Star Wars figures still in their boxes, all of which conspire to push the car out of the garage and into the front yard. Add in a few bags of trash that can't find their way to the curb for pickup, and the next thing anyone knows, the people residing in the house are trapped. Most end up sleeping on top of a pile of dirty clothes because they can no longer find their beds. Of course the situation wouldn't have gotten so bad if their army of non-neutered cats hadn't continued to spawn new litters of kittens.

Before the occupants knew what happened, their house became a mewing, mildewy, macabre mess, a mess you'd think they'd love to be rescued from, but no! When a concerned family member tries to remove so much as a cobweb, the trapped inhabitant protests, "But that's Sylvia, my favorite spider. I couldn't possibly part with her. Her work has been hanging on my walls for years!"

But by the end of the show, after a professional cleanup team sorts through the massive contents of the house, clears away the carcasses of a few expired pets, and hauls away the trash, a miracle happens. With their belongings no longer piled to the ceiling, the homeowners walk from room to room admiring the fact that, yes, their house does have a floor, and even a couch you can sit on! One woman gushes, "I have so much space that I can now open my refrigerator door!" while a man admits, "With the hallways passable, I don't have to use the outdoor toilet in the backyard." Another amazed homeowner looks around at her now livable space and says, "I had no idea I'd let things get so bad."

Really? You didn't notice the smell of your dead pets or that you had to climb over a mountain of clothes and newspapers to get to the kitchen?

Somehow, I believe their admission of blindness because I've seen this same blindness at work in my own life.

While my family is not buried under a pile of old newspapers, my office has been known to contain so many piles of books that you'd think the local library had opened a branch on my desk. Being a book lover and a card-carrying member of the media, I receive books in the mail every week—beautiful books, signed-by-author books, and books I absolutely love and could not possibly part with. That is, until my piles of books got so big that my office became little more than a book storage facility.

Afraid that a pile of books could fall and hurt someone, I finally decided to do something about it. Two of my friends and I spent an entire day sorting my books—some to keep but the majority to give to a prison ministry. The good news is that by letting go of so many of my treasured books not only was I able to encourage prisoners and their wives, but I was also able to reclaim my office. How wonderful it was to return to my desk and work on my projects.

So as someone who's had her own struggles with hoarding, I feel somewhat of a connection to those A&E hoarders and therefore feel I have the right to discuss their issues. It seems to me that life is about figuring out which things should be discarded and which things should be kept and put in their rightful place. This same wisdom can be applied to the things that overwhelm us.

I think a lot of people are paralyzed by worry, grief, and fear, or, in other words, they've reached the point where they are overwhelmed.

According to my research, the word *overwhelm* has several meanings. Tap your finger next to any that apply to how you are feeling:

1. To overcome completely in mind or feeling.
2. To overpower or overcome, especially with superior forces; destroy; crush.
3. To cover or bury beneath a mass of something, as floodwaters, debris, or an avalanche; submerge.
4. To load, heap, treat, or address with an overpowering or excessive amount of anything.[1]

Most of these definitions could be applied to the hoarders we discussed earlier as well as to ourselves as we struggle to sort through our own messes.

Trying to deal with your messes may be what inspired you to pick up this book. You're looking for power to help you cope or even to change your circumstances. If so, I'm really excited for you. You're headed for a breakthrough—a breakthrough where you'll clean up your soul by learning how to let go of your toxic emotions and yield to the peace of the Holy Spirit. But it's going to take some work on your part, as you're going to have to:

- clean house
- let go of your control
- learn how to be dependent on God

Clean House

As many a reformed hoarder can tell you, housecleaning is not without its rewards. As we dig out of our messes, we might even find a treasure or two. For example, as I was rearranging my remaining books on my bookshelves, I found a solid gold coin that my son had placed on that shelf fourteen years earlier.

Jim and I had studied coin collecting the one semester I'd homeschooled him when he was nine years old. The lesson on coins had led to a field trip to our town's coin shop, where we'd placed a low-ball bid on this coin in an auction. To our delight, we won the coin for a song. But somehow, instead of putting it away when we got home, we placed the coin on the bookshelf and forgot about it. Fourteen years later, I uncovered the treasure, now worth hundreds more than what we'd paid for it.

Cleaning out our lives is a lot like my experience of cleaning out my office. Not only will taking out your emotional trash give you more "livable" space, but you'll also discover forgotten treasures like peace, a treasure far more valuable than a gold coin.

Another treasure I gleaned from cleaning out my books was the knowledge that I'd put idle resources to good use—investing my dusty books in the lives of men and women who needed them. In fact, the ministry soon wrote to say, "Linda, you should have seen the faces of the wives of the prisoners when we handed out the books and CDs you sent to them. Each resource was a perfect fit for the one who received it."

I'm wondering what resources and treasures have been locked inside you because of the emotional congestion in your heart and soul?

Don't be afraid to invite Jesus in to take inventory of your life, to sort through your difficulties, and to sweep out the cobwebs. Like the professional cleaners who rescued those hoarders on A&E, Jesus comes to remove our trash—our sins, shame, stress, and feelings of being overwhelmed by our present troubles and trials.

The good news is that we are about to start the process of cleaning out our toxic emotions in our upcoming times of yielding prayer. As you pray with me, not only will you find the treasure of supernatural peace, but you'll also experience supernatural joy as you fully trust God to lead you through your difficulties.

Let Go of Your Control

"But," you might complain, "don't you see? I would never have to deal with toxic emotions if I could control all of the troublesome areas of my life."

You do have an interesting point. Imagine what it would be like if you *were* in perfect control of all that concerns you. Whenever you wanted to drop a couple of pounds, the extra weight would vanish by lunchtime. Or you could instantly cure cancer with a knowing smile or create an extra payday just by wishing. If you could accomplish these things by yourself, do you think your abilities would lead you to trust God more deeply, or would you be tempted to trust more fully in yourself?

Perhaps the reason we aren't the answer to our every problem is that we would never discover the truth behind Romans 8:28: "And we know that in all things God works for the good of those who love him, who have been called according to his purpose."

Think about it. If everything always went our way, how would we ever discover that God can flip our difficulties into good, like the time a cancer patient didn't find his complete healing until he discovered he was cancer-free in heaven? Or the time a jilted fiancée discovered her true love to be someone she met *because* God ignored her original prayer to be reunited with the one who broke her heart?

So perhaps instead of kidding ourselves into believing we can become the boss of our own circumstances, much less the boss of God, we need to learn how to trust God more deeply than we ever thought possible—even when we don't understand what God is doing or why.

Sarah Young shared wise words in her devotional *Jesus Calling*, written from the perspective of Christ. "When you start to feel stressed, let those feelings alert you to your need for Me. . . . Thank Me for the difficulties in your life as they provide protection from the idolatry of self-reliance."[2] In other words, it's like Jesus said in John 15:5: "I am the vine; you are the branches. If you remain in me and I in you, you will bear much fruit; apart from me you can do nothing." If we are "in Christ," not only will we not be overwhelmed by our trials, but we will also be fruitful and victorious.

Learn How to Be Dependent on God

We were created to be continually dependent on God, yet we often strive for our independence. We're like a toddler who manages to aim a gallon jug of milk at a small glass on the edge of the kitchen table. When her fingers slip, this little one unleashes an ice-cold tidal wave that cascades across the table, down her dress, and into her tennis shoes before sloshing across the floor. If only this child had allowed her loving father to help, she could have tasted the milk instead of wearing it.

This little girl reminds me of us as we desperately try to control our own lives with an "I can do it myself" mentality. But too often our circumstances slip from our grasp to splatter into a massive mess, and we're left to mop up. That's when we look up to ask the Almighty, "Were you just standing there watching when my life turned into this mess? Don't you even care?"

Instead of scolding God, we should humbly seek more than his help; we should seek to become dependent on him. After all, God is our loving heavenly Father who's standing by, ready to turn our messes into miracles. However, when we seek his guidance, we'll avoid the messes altogether, just as when a child allows her dad to pour her milk.

We need to be like the psalmist David, who cried, "In my distress I called to the LORD; I cried to my God for help. From his temple he heard my voice; my cry came before him, into his ears" (Ps. 18:6).

The Story of Peace Continued

Take a moment to go back in time, as David's life became a nightmare.

David bent toward the low mouth of the cave, then scrambled in on his hands and knees. Long moments passed until he found room enough to sit up and lean against a damp rock. He blinked in the inky darkness, barely believing it had come to this—crawling into what could easily become his tomb. David pulled out a small harp from the sack he'd lugged along and strummed his thumb over its strings. A jarring chord echoed on the walls around him, and suddenly he felt overwhelmed.

It hadn't even been a year since he'd lopped off the head of the giant Goliath to win a much needed victory for the Israelite army. But the trouble had started as he accompanied King Saul on their victory march back to the palace. In every town they entered, Saul would hold up Goliath's head by its hair as the women danced in the streets and sang, "Saul has slain his thousands, but David his tens of thousands." At first King Saul only laughed at the lyrics, but as the song became the unofficial anthem of the people, a cloud fell over his face, a cloud that continued to darken.

Sometime later, after Saul had called David back to the palace, the storm finally erupted as David played his harp for the king. As David sang, Saul closed his eyes and listened until his smile twisted. The king's sword struck the wall as David leapt, barely escaping death.

Three more times the king missed his mark. But when David learned of Saul's plot to kill him, he knew it was time to run for his life—to retreat to this old hiding place, only a stone's throw from where he'd faced down Goliath.

How far he'd fallen!

As David pondered these things, he tuned his harp, confident he was far enough into the cave so as not to be heard. The tuning complete, David closed his eyes and sang from his heart:

> I cry out to the LORD;
>> I plead for the LORD's mercy.
> I pour out my complaints before him
>> and tell him all my troubles.
> When I am overwhelmed,
>> you alone know the way I should turn.

Wherever I go,
    my enemies have set traps for me.

David wiped his eyes on his sleeve and continued to sing his sorrow:

I look for someone to come and help me,
    but no one gives me a passing thought!
No one will help me;
    no one cares a bit what happens to me. (Ps. 142:1–4 NLT)

David's thoughts wandered to all that had happened since he'd become the hero of the land. His own family had pulled away from him, in part because they felt his success should have belonged to his older brothers. Then, in his flight from the palace, he'd been forced to leave his best friend, Jonathan, behind. It would not be fitting for the son of the king to go into hiding with him.

Then there was the beautiful Michal with her dark, flowing hair and her liquid green eyes. She was Saul's daughter, whom David had taken as his wife—despite the fact that he'd known his betrothal to her was merely one of Saul's baited traps. Saul's face had registered shock when David had strolled into his court with the demanded dowry, bloody proof that he had indeed slain one hundred Philistine men as a payment for his bride.

But now, despite all his triumphs, he was alone, with only his Lord to talk to. David continued his song:

Then I pray to you, O LORD.
    I say, "You are my place of refuge.
    You are all I really want in life.

Hear my cry,
    for I am very low.
Rescue me from my persecutors,
    for they are too strong for me.
Bring me out of prison
    so I can thank you.
The godly will crowd around me,
    for you are good to me."
       (Ps. 142:5–7 NLT)
       (based on 1 Sam. 18–19, 22)

What a prayer! In the lowest place in his life, a place where David admitted to being unimaginably overwhelmed, he called out to the Lord to thank him for his goodness. Don't you think that if David could find this kind of peace despite his circumstances you can too? Yes, and we'll work toward this goal of peace together. But in the meantime, you may be wondering what ever became of David as he hid in the cave.

It's good news. God heard David's prayers and moved on his behalf. His family came to be with him—their relationship restored. His parents and brothers were soon followed by four hundred mighty men who wanted to stand with David against Saul. This meant that later, when he hid in the caverns and strummed his lyre, he sang not only to praise God but also to encourage those God had sent to stand with him.

Shine the Light of the Word

While David became the leader of a small army, he stayed on the lam for many years, managing to stay just out of King Saul's grasp. But throughout his troubles, he began to notice a pattern.

Whenever he called upon the Lord, the Lord showed up—freeing him from whatever trap Saul had set. David continued to lament his trouble before the Lord, but he always ended his laments with strong statements of praise and trust, as he did in Psalm 31:24: "Be of good courage, and He shall strengthen your heart, all you who hope in the LORD" (NKJV).

You too can take David's hard-learned truth to heart, but first pray, "Lord, open my eyes to see your truth as I read Psalm 31:24 again."

Write down your thoughts and impressions regarding how this Scripture passage might apply to you:

_____

_____

_____

_____

Review what you gleaned and thank God for these truths.

Now we are going to pray not only a prayer of hope but also a prayer that will help us yield all of our feelings of being overwhelmed to the Holy Spirit. In this way, we will exchange our stress for the supernatural peace of Christ. After all, Jesus is the Prince of Peace who came to give us peace. It's time that we learned how to receive this peace through the workings of the Holy Spirit.

Yielding Prayer for the Overwhelmed

To start the process and to yield to the peace of the Holy Spirit, we're going to use prayer. Much like the A&E hoarders, we're going to call on someone outside ourselves (in this case, God, who is a pro at this sort of thing) to declutter our hearts and to remove the piles of stress that threaten to overwhelm us.

Shine the Light

Dear Lord,
Please turn on your light of truth over me and my feelings of being overwhelmed. Show me which attitudes you would like to set me free from so we can clean my soul and make more room for you and your peace.

List the situations that have overwhelmed you:

_____

_____

_____

_____

Yield

Put your hand over your stomach and pray the following:

Dear Lord,
I yield all these things, including my feelings of being overwhelmed, to your peace through your Holy Spirit.

With your hand still on your stomach, take deep breaths and start to relax as you repeat the prayer above until you feel God's peace drop into your spirit.

Forgive

Dear Lord,

I'm not strong enough to let go and forgive myself, you, and those who have caused me distress in any of these areas. Still, I choose to forgive. Therefore, I ask that you, through your Holy Spirit inside me, forgive all. I acknowledge that you, Lord, are without sin. Though you may have allowed these difficulties, you will use them as seeds for miracles. Thank you!

Give It All to God

Dear Lord,

I cast these situations at the foot of the cross. Now they are your problems, not mine. Thank you for setting me free from feeling overwhelmed.

Pray for Healing

Dear Lord,

Please heal the pain caused by my feelings of being overwhelmed. Thank you for your supernatural peace.

Exchange the Enemy's Work for God's Peace

Dear Lord,

Please forgive me for allowing my circumstances to overwhelm me instead of trusting in you. I close all the doors I have opened to the enemy in this area. In addition, I cancel any plans the enemy has for my life. I cast out any power or influence from any evil spirits trying to overwhelm me. I pray this in the power of the name and blood of Jesus.

I exchange the enemy's work for God's peace. Send the river of your peace not only to me but also to those overwhelmed by these same influences and circumstances. I pray this also in the power of the name and blood of Jesus.

Praise God—You Are Free!

Thank you, Lord! I'm free!

Pray this prayer whenever you need a redo.

3

Stuck

Finding Release from the Cares of This World

> He makes me strong again. He leads me in the
> way of living right with Himself which brings
> honor to His name.
>
> Psalm 23:3 NLV

As the lambs leapt about, the fat ewe looked up from the rich clover she'd been munching, then wandered toward the shady oak for a nap. As she nestled her pregnant belly on the cool earth, the weight of her wool and the slope of the ground caused her to roll over, her four legs scrambling at the sky. Try as she might, she could not flip over. She was stuck on her back!

The old English shepherds would say this sheep was "cast down." This sheep's compromised position put her in danger of being attacked by a coyote. But even if a coyote failed to attack, the ewe and the lamb she was carrying would be dead in a matter of hours because of the pressures of the gases building within her, a terrible loss to the shepherd.

Perhaps you can relate. You know how it feels to be cast down or stuck—rolled over and pinned down by the pressures of this world. If you feel as if you've fallen and can't get up, let me encourage you to *look* up, because the Good Shepherd is on his way. You don't need to press a panic button. All you need to do is call out to Jesus. He is never too late. He will arrive in time to help get you back on your feet.

Phillip Keller, who wrote *A Shepherd Looks at Psalm 23*, was once a shepherd himself. When he tended sheep, if he saw a vulture's slow circle, he knew that one of his sheep was in trouble, and he'd immediately race to the rescue. When he found a cast down sheep, he'd gently roll it over on its side to relieve the building gases. After a while, he'd stand the sheep upright and rub circulation back into its legs until it could take a wobbly step. Then, after the sheep revived enough to regain its equilibrium, he would watch as it dashed away to join the others.

Keller says:

> Many people have the idea that when a child of God fails, when he is frustrated and helpless in a spiritual dilemma, God becomes disgusted, fed up and even furious with him.
>
> This simply is not so.
>
> One of the greatest revelations of the heart of God given to us by Christ is that of Himself as our Shepherd. He has the same identical sensations of anxiety, concern and compassion for cast men and women as I had for cast sheep. This is precisely why He looked on people with such pathos and compassion.[1]

Keller is right. We have a Good Shepherd who cares if we're cast down or entangled by the traps, snares, or cares of this world. But when you're stuck, it can be hard to know what to do to get back up. If you should find yourself in such a predicament, you can find God's freedom when you:

- till the soil of your heart
- look for God's peace
- shine the light of God's truth into your situation

Till the Soil of Your Heart

The cares of this world—like problems, the constant pursuit of more, the sting of loss, as well as unending busyness—can be as dangerous to us as thorns are to a sheep that becomes cast down in thorny brambles.

Jesus told a story to warn of thorny dangers when he spoke to a crowd gathered along the shore of Galilee. As he used the stern of Peter's boat for a pulpit, he told of a farmer who went out to sow his seeds. Jesus explained:

> And as he sowed, some seeds fell on the path, and the birds came and ate them up. Other seeds fell on rocky ground, where they did not have much soil, and they sprang up quickly, since they had no depth of soil. But when the sun rose, they were scorched; and since they had no root, they withered away. Other seeds fell among thorns, and the thorns grew up and choked them. Other seeds fell on good soil and brought forth grain, some a hundredfold, some sixty, some thirty. Let anyone with ears listen! (Matt. 13:4–9 NRSV)

At these words, Peter probably raised an eyebrow at the other disciples as if to say, "Whatever is the Master talking about?"

Later that evening, probably as the men poked around the campfire they had built on the beach, the disciples asked Jesus to explain his story. Jesus said:

> When anyone hears the word of the kingdom and does not understand it, the evil one comes and snatches away what is sown in the heart; this is what was sown on the path. As for what was sown on rocky ground, this is the one who hears the word and immediately receives it with joy; yet such a person has no root, but endures only for a while, and when trouble or persecution arises on account of the word, that person immediately falls away. As for what was sown among thorns, this is the one who hears the word, but the cares of the world and the lure of wealth choke the word, and it yields nothing. But as for what was sown on good soil, this is the one who hears the word and understands it, who indeed bears fruit and yields, in one case a hundredfold, in another sixty, and in another thirty. (Matt. 13:19–23 NRSV)

According to Jesus's explanation, not everyone who hears the Word is able to receive it, hold on to it, or grow in it. The problems that can prevent a person from doing these things include:

- lack of understanding the truth
- not allowing the Word to take root
- giving in to the cares of this world

But those who do receive the Word and grow in it can produce a harvest that helps others. How does this happen? According to Jesus's parable, it has to do with the quality of the soil.

What's the quality of the soil in your heart, your dwelling for the Holy Spirit? Are you pursuing truth and allowing it to take root, or are the thorns of stress, worries, and striving for riches preventing you from yielding to the peace God is ready to supply? As Paul said in Philippians, "And the peace of God, which transcends all understanding, will guard your hearts and your minds in Christ Jesus" (4:7).

To prevent soil problems, till the soil of your soul so that God's Word can take root. Then his peace will help you grow and reproduce, no matter the floods or storms that come your way. Dig up the stones of unbelief as well as the thorns of stress and desires for riches. With your permission and cooperation, God will work the soil of your heart, and your life will become a lovely garden for him.

Look for God's Peace

Proverbs 4:23 says, "Keep your heart with all diligence, for out of it spring the issues of life" (NKJV). I love this Scripture passage because it reminds me that though God freely gave me the gift of forgiveness through his Son as well as the indwelling of the Holy Spirit, he expects me to diligently keep my heart—yielding my messes to the Holy Spirit so I can live a more powerful, stress-free life.

One of my favorite quotations from the devotional *Dear Jesus* is, "I have poured My very Being into you, in the person of the Holy Spirit. Make plenty of room in your heart for this glorious One."[2] Making more room in our hearts for the Holy Spirit will empower us to live in peace.

But don't be fooled. Peace is not passive; it's powerful. The enemy cannot stand against us when we are standing in the peace of Christ. When we take away the enemy's weapons of fear and stress, he has little left with which to attack us. Plus, standing in the peace of God will give us the power to shine the light on the barrier of darkness that the enemy tries to place between us and the Holy Spirit.

Shine the Light of God's Truth into Your Situation

I read an article about how scientists were impeding light to mask objects and events. It wasn't until I chatted with a friend that I came to understand the deep spiritual implications of this research. Kathi told me about the great spiritual darkness in the town where she lives. She said, "There's so much spiritual darkness in this area that it seems to mask God's truth," and the light dawned.

I returned to the article I'd read in *Nature, International Weekly Journal of Science* to review the report that scientists at Cornell University had in essence created "invisibility." They'd been able to impede part of a beam of light so that it bent to cloak an event, if only for a nanosecond.[3] Journalist Katie Drummond described the results of this experiment this way:

> Masking an object entails bending light around that object. If the light doesn't actually hit an object, then that object won't be visible to the human eye. . . . Where events are

concerned, concealment relies on changing the speed of light. Light that's emitted from actions, as they happen, is what allows us to see those actions happen. Usually, that light comes in a constant flow. What Cornell researchers did, in simple terms, is tweak that ongoing flow of light—just for a mere iota of time—so that an event could transpire without being observable.[4]

I think that's exactly what the enemy, the ruler of darkness, does to us—he impedes the light of God's truth in our lives, even if only for a nanosecond, just enough to distort or hide God's grace, mercy, joy, peace, and love from us. Although these gifts are constantly available to us, when God's light is impeded, we may not see them.

But thank God that we can turn on the light when we focus on Jesus. Second Corinthians 4:6 says, "For God, who said, 'Let there be light in the darkness,' has made this light shine in our hearts so we could know the glory of God that is seen in the face of Jesus Christ" (NLT).

Now you know why we start our yielding prayer time by praying that God's unimpeded light will shine over the situations we are bringing to him. We know that the light of Christ will prevent the enemy from cloaking even an iota of God's truth so that the enemy cannot hide any of the gifts God has for us. As God's light shines in our lives, our blind spots disappear, and unlike the A&E hoarders, we'll be able not only to see the mess we made but also God helping us clean it up. We'll be set free from darkness as we enjoy even more of God's presence and peace in our lives.

Plus, God's light will help us see a great truth that the enemy wants us to miss, namely, that God is a God we can trust. Hebrews 10:35 says, "So do not throw away this confident trust in the Lord. Remember the great reward it brings you!" (NLT).

The Story of Peace Continued

It was the peace that comes from trusting in Jesus that Peter and the disciples lost while in a terrible storm.

Peter and his brother Andrew set the sails of their boat and caught a breeze that whisked Jesus as well as the disciples away from the throng on the beach.

Peter gave a worried glance at the Master, who'd spent the day teaching in the blazing sun. Peter pointed to a protected place on the stern. "Master, why not rest as we set for the far shore?"

Jesus smiled and gave Peter a nod before laying his head on the cushion Peter had placed there. Jesus was soon asleep, despite a sudden sprinkle of rain.

Peter watched as the setting sun turned the bellies of the heavy clouds ablaze with pink and orange and said to Andrew, "I don't like the looks of that sky."

Andrew kidded him. "Where's your mustard seed of faith that the Master spoke of this afternoon?"

Peter's brow furrowed. "I have no need for a mustard tree at the moment, but a clear sky and a calm sea would give me all the confidence I need."

As the darkness deepened, the clouds began to crackle with flashes that lit them from the inside out. The crackles soon turned into jagged streaks of lightning, while booms of thunder beat the sky like a drum. Peter felt his boat shudder as the wind churned the sea to swells. He gave a quick glance at Jesus. How could he sleep through this?

The storm turned ugly as the boat ascended a high crest before plunging to the bottom of the swell as a mighty wave splashed over the crew.

"Shouldn't we wake the Master?" Andrew asked Peter. "The boat's taking on water."

"Why haven't you wakened him already," Thomas called above the wind as he stumbled toward them. "Don't you think Jesus would want to know we are all about to *die*?"

Peter shook the Master. "Why are you sleeping? Don't you care that we're going to drown?"

Jesus sat up and looked out at the blackened sea as the wind and rain pelted his face. He stood and held out his hands and simply commanded, "Peace, be still!" The wind stopped, and the boat glided into a great calm.

Peter was stunned as he looked at the placid sea.

Jesus turned to his disciples. "Why are you so afraid? Don't you have any faith?"

As the men went back to their duties, Andrew's voice was laced with fear as he whispered to Peter, "Who is this man who can calm the wind and the seas?"

All Peter could do was shake his head and wonder, "Who indeed?" (based on Mark 4:35–41).

Who is he? Simply put, Jesus is Lord! He's the one we can trust as we give him not only our lives but also our concerns.

Jesus can calm our storms and give us peace, as he demonstrated inside the storm.

Shine the Light of the Word

We, like the disciples, can get stuck in our fear when we do not trust God in our storms. Let's see what Philippians 4:6–7 has to say to help us break free: "Do not be anxious about anything, but in every situation, by prayer and petition, with thanksgiving, present your requests to God. And the peace of God, which transcends all understanding, will guard your hearts and your minds in Christ Jesus."

Say this simple prayer: "Open my eyes to your truth as I read Philippians 4:6–7 again."

Write down your thoughts and impressions regarding how this Scripture passage might apply to you:

_____

_____

_____

Review what you gleaned and thank God for these truths.

Yielding Prayer for the Stuck

If the traps, snares, and cares of this world have such a grip on your life that you feel stuck in stress and worry, it's time to turn on the light of truth. In this light, you can see that you serve not only a God you can trust but also a God who is waiting to give you gifts of peace, favor, and joy.

Shine the Light

Dear Lord,
 Please turn on your light of truth over me and my stress.
Reveal any areas where I doubt your provision or plan for
my life or areas where I am striving outside of your peace.

List the situations of unbelief and strife that the Lord is
revealing to you:

_____

_____

_____

_____

Yield

Put your hand over your stomach and pray the following:

Dear Lord,
 I yield all these things, including my focus on the trap
of the cares of this world, to your peace through your Holy
Spirit.

With your hand still on your stomach, take deep breaths
and start to relax as you repeat the prayer above until you
feel God's peace drop into your spirit.

Forgive

Dear Lord,
 I'm not strong enough to let go and forgive myself, you,
and those who have caused me distress in any of these areas.

Still, I choose to forgive. Therefore, I ask that you, through your Holy Spirit inside me, forgive all. I acknowledge that you, Lord, are without sin. Though you may have allowed these difficulties, you will use them as seeds for miracles. Thank you!

Give It All to God

Dear Lord,

I cast my cares at the foot of the cross. Now they are your cares, not mine. Thank you for setting me free from striving and stress in these areas.

Pray for Healing

Dear Lord,

Please heal the pain caused by the trap of the cares of this world. Thank you for your supernatural peace.

Exchange the Enemy's Work for God's Peace

Dear Lord,

Please forgive me for bowing before the trap of the cares of this world. I close all the doors I have opened to the enemy in this area. In addition, I cancel any plans the enemy has for my life. I cast out any power or influence from any evil spirits trying to trap me in my striving to satisfy my desires instead of trusting in God. I pray this in the power of the name and blood of Jesus.

I exchange the enemy's work for God's peace. Send the river of your peace not only to me but also to those with whom I've been striving regarding my cares, needs, and wants. I pray this also in the power of the name and blood of Jesus.

Praise God—You Are Free!

Thank you, Lord! I'm free!

Pray this prayer whenever you need a redo.

4

Frustrated

Finding Contentment in Difficulties

But let patience have its perfect work, that you
may be perfect and complete, lacking nothing.

James 1:4 NKJV

If I asked you if there was ever a time you felt frustrated,
perhaps you'd say, "Yeah, try my entire life."

Life *is* frustrating. It seems we spend a lot of time annoyed
or upset because we cannot change our lives or achieve all that
is in our hearts because of our limitations, difficult people,
or circumstances.

Trust me, I know. I've been there too.

When my then eighteen-month-old daughter was injured
in a terrible car accident, even before the ambulance arrived,
I knelt beside her in the middle of the freeway and prayed

to God for her life. I begged God, "Please bring Laura back to me. Don't let her die!"

It seemed as if God not only ignored my cry but was also determined to give Laura neither life nor death, for Laura hovered for days, then weeks, and finally months in a state of unconsciousness.

But I had hope. The doctors in the Texas Catholic ICU told me that the doctors in Colorado had a coma-stimulation program that would surely pull Laura back to the land of the living. So when we arrived in Denver by air ambulance, three months into our ordeal, I was excited to see how God would answer my constant prayers.

The next several weeks were busy as the staff poked, prodded, and gave my daughter every conceivable test. Then came the day of the big reveal, and I was anxious to hear the plan. But instead of telling me how they were going to wake my daughter up, twenty-six health care professionals surrounded me to say, "Laura's not in a coma; she's in a vegetative state. She'll never wake up."

Their prognosis?

Hopeless.

One doctor put it this way: "Your daughter could live in this vegetative state until she's eighty years old."

I was so shocked that when the meeting ended I walked out of the room as if I were a zombie. But in the coming days, my shock turned to determination. I would continue to call out to God for help. My only comfort was the knowledge that my God was bigger than the hospital staff's prognosis.

A week later, one of the doctors slipped into Laura's hospital room to confide in me. "I have good news. Because of your daughter's head injury, it's unlikely she will grow taller.

She will stay about the size she is today. That means she'll be easy for you to manage."

My face flamed with frustration. "Number one," I said, keeping my voice low and steady, "what makes you think this is good news, and number two, scientifically speaking, you can't tell the difference between a coma and a vegetative state. So if we put God in the equation, how do you know Laura won't get better?"

The doctor kept his eyes locked on mine as he backed toward the door. "Oh, I didn't know you were in denial," he accused before he turned and fled.

That's when the hospital chaplain got involved. She soon knocked on Laura's door. "Come in," I said, glad she'd finally come to pray with me.

The chaplain said, "I understand that you think your daughter can get better."

I answered cautiously, "Yes, I do."

"Can you tell me why?"

I tilted my head toward my sleeping daughter. "Have you seen her? She can't get much worse."

The chaplain frowned but looked determined to get me under control. "I understand that you think your daughter can get better because of God. Is this true?"

That's when it dawned on me. The chaplain and I weren't playing ball for the same team.

I gave my chin a slight jut. "Yes."

"And you're basing that on the Bible?" she asked, as if ready for a debate.

"Yes," I answered again.

Her eyes held me prisoner. "Can you tell me exactly where in the Bible?"

I broke her spell as I crossed my arms and said, "Try the whole Bible."

The gleam in the chaplain's eyes told me she thought that I was a lot worse than she'd suspected. But she wasn't through with her intervention. Her visit was followed by social workers who all seemed bent on making me recant my "My daughter can get better because of God" theory. But as frustrated as I was with the ongoing crisis, I wouldn't recant.

Yet, in the dark days and nights that followed, I continued to hover over my precious child and saw very little evidence to validate my stubbornly held position. Except for an occasional smile or a flutter of an eyelash, it seemed as if my daughter had left her body and was visiting some place very far away from her hospital bed.

Into the wee hours of the night I would cry out to God in frustration. "Why won't you answer my prayers? Why won't you return my daughter to me? Don't you love me? Don't you care that the entire staff of this hospital thinks I've lost it?"

Hopefully, you've never had a loved one in this kind of situation. But I share my story with you so that you'll know I really do understand what it means to be frustrated. Before I tell you the rest of this story, I want to take a break and explore how you can tame your feelings of frustration and live with contentment regardless of your circumstances. Take a deep breath, then consider that you can:

- give God your frustrations
- trust God in your frustrations
- develop a grateful heart

Give God Your Frustrations

One of Max Lucado's readers asked him, "Why talk to God about my troubles? He can't understand."[1]

Lucado referred this man to Hebrews 4:15, where it says, "For we do not have a high priest who is unable to empathize with our weaknesses, but we have one who has been tempted in every way, just as we are—yet he did not sin."

Yes! Even when I felt alone in my daughter's hospital room, not only was God with me, but he also cared and even understood how I felt.

If you've ever wondered if God cares or understands your feelings, consider this Lucado remark:

> Every page of the Gospels hammers home this crucial principle: God knows how you feel. From the funeral to the factory to the frustration of a demanding schedule, Jesus understands. When you tell God that you've reached your limit, he knows what you mean. When you shake your head at impossible deadlines, he shakes his head too. When your plans are interrupted by people who have other plans, he nods in empathy.
>
> He has been there.
> He knows how you feel.[2]

Lucado is right. God not only knows how we feel but also cares. Plus, God knows how to help us and give us strength. Philippians 4:13 reminds us, "I can do all this through him who gives me strength."

When my daughter was hurt in our terrible accident, I was a young mom who'd never stood up to an authority figure. But God empowered me to stand against the will of an entire hospital. Looking back, I can tell you that God was with me, keeping me strong even though my heart was breaking.

Today, I can tell you that when your heart is breaking, when you are feeling harassment or the pain of frustration, God wants to help. He wants you to place the weight of all that you're carrying, all the pain that you're feeling, into his loving hands, which undergird your own.

Pray this simple prayer:

Lord,

I believe you do know how I feel and that you care. As you can see, my hands are full of so much that frustrates me. Thank you that your hands are beneath mine, holding my hands up, even giving me the strength I need to overcome. I now drop the contents of what I've been trying to carry myself into your capable hands. Thank you that I can rest in you.

In Jesus's name, amen.

Trust God in Your Frustrations

I knew I was in a terrible dance with the hospital staff. If they could get me to admit that God was not a party to our situation, that my daughter's fate rested solely in my own hands, the conclusion would be simple: euthanasia—allowing my daughter to die by starvation.

Help me, God! Help me stand up to this threat. Lord, if you want to take Laura home to yourself, you have my permission. I trust you to make that decision on Laura's behalf.

Sometimes I would place my lips to my daughter's ear. "If Jesus asks, it's okay to stay in heaven with him. Mommy will be okay." But somehow, despite the ever present threat of death, Laura continued to survive.

You may be wondering, *In the midst of such frustrations, how is it possible to trust God?*

Billy Graham once said, "Doubts are a normal part of life. We doubt things on earth, so it's easy to doubt the things of God. Yet God's promises are His promises. What He has said in the past remains true today. God never changes or goes back on His Word. If He did, then He wouldn't be God."[3]

Trusting God is a choice, and once we choose to trust him, God himself will guard that trust. It's like Paul said when he wrote Timothy about his own trials, "That is why I am suffering as I am. Yet this is no cause for shame, because I know whom I have believed, and am convinced that he is able to guard what I have entrusted to him until that day" (2 Tim. 1:12).

But you might ask, "What about the times God fails to answer that which I've trusted him to do?"

Graham put it this way: "It's true that God often doesn't come through in the way and timing you expected, but that's not a flaw in God; it's a flaw in your expectations."[4] In other words, God has his own ways of doing things, ways that will lead to miracles you may not have anticipated. The key is to trust him to do the thing that will bring the most good, even when you don't have a clue what he's up to.

Pray this:

Dear Lord,
 I choose to trust you, even when you're not doing things the way I've asked. When this happens, despite all appear-

ances, I know you are working a greater miracle. I also know that you will guard my trust and help me through.

In Jesus's name, amen.

Develop a Grateful Heart

Stormie Omartian shares about the time she and her family moved to Tennessee from California and experienced what she was later told was a one-hundred-year ice storm. Ice coated everything—streets, houses, cars, and unfortunately power and phone lines. Stuck inside their house, her family wasn't going anywhere, except to huddle around the fireplace. Their ordeal stretched on day after day. In her fear, she sought the Lord. "Lord, help us. We need to know You're here."

She said, "I immediately sensed that instead of despairing over the misery of the situation, I was to embrace the experience and find His goodness in it. As I did, the results surprised me. I thanked God that He had kept us together as a family, instead of having someone stranded elsewhere and not knowing if they were safe. I was grateful that He had prepared us with a good supply of food and bottled water. I appreciated our fireplace and warm clothes that kept us from freezing. . . . Our bodies were cold, but our hearts were warmed by the light He gave our souls."[5]

Omartian got it. She was able to discover the miracle within her ordeal by being grateful.

Oftentimes, God keeps his ways a secret, but when we have a grateful heart, God may open our eyes so we can see the joy we might have otherwise missed.

The best way to develop a grateful heart is to learn how to walk in step with God. Omartian explains, "Walking step by step with God requires embracing the moment for all it's worth. When you are tempted to become fearful, frustrated, uncertain, or panicked about what is happening in your life, stop and see that God is in it. And with Him, you have everything you need for this moment. Here and now."[6]

Let's pray:

Dear Lord,
    Remind me that you are in the moment, even the moments that frustrate me. Help me to learn how to walk in step with you so I can develop a grateful heart and see you at work. I choose peace and contentment regardless of what I'm going through.
    In Jesus's name, amen.

The Story of Peace Continued

The biblical story I am about to share is about a woman so frustrated by her circumstances that she tried to bypass God and take matters into her own hands. See how her hard-won lessons apply to you.

My arms longed for the baby my husband, Abraham, told me the Lord had promised me. For years I waited, watching as our herds and slaves produced enough offspring to repopulate the city of Ur, yet my arms remained empty. As I was long past my childbearing years, I felt frustrated. How could God fulfill his promise that Abraham would become the father of many nations unless I myself intervened?

That's when I decided to do what a lot of women in my situation did. I gave my husband Hagar, my own attendant.

My plan was to raise the child of their union as my own, but as Hagar's belly swelled, she was not so easy to convince. She explained in my tent, "Sarah, you forget that I am the mother of Abraham's child, not you."

I blinked back tears as Hagar swept away a lock of her dark, silky hair and declared, "By the right of my child's birth, I will no longer be treated as a slave in this household. You will soon honor me as I stand with my child beside Abraham."

With Hagar trying to take my place, I was more frustrated than ever and furious that my plan had backfired. I blamed my husband for this mess and told him so. "You are responsible for the wrong I am suffering. I put my slave in your arms, and now that she knows she is pregnant, she despises me. May the Lord judge between you and me."

How relieved I was when Abraham took my side. "Do with her what you want," he'd instructed.

I treated Hagar so harshly that she did what I'd hoped; she ran away into the desert. I thought I'd never see her or her offspring again, but she returned, though with a better attitude about her place as my servant.

The years ticked by, and her son, Ishmael, was thirteen years old when my husband entertained three strangers in our tent. As I stood near the tent flap, I heard one of the guests tell Abraham, "I will surely return to you about this time next year, and Sarah, your wife, will have a son."

I closed my eyes and covered my mouth with my hand, trying to shoo away the laughter that begged to dance into the evening air. I guess our guest hadn't a clue I was in my nineties.

My giggles stopped when one of the guests asked, "Why did Sarah laugh and say, 'Will I really have a child, now that I am old?'"

This stranger had read my thoughts. Then he stunned me by saying, "Is anything too hard for the Lord?"

Despite my years of barrenness, God's words proved true. Here, let me lift the blanket. See how peacefully he sleeps? Isaac, the child of my laughter, born out of years of frustration, the spiritual heir of both my husband and myself. Here is the child of promise—at long last (based on Gen. 16–18, 21).

Manipulation, blame, anger, deception, and cruelty were key parts of Sarah's story, but none of these behaviors got her what she wanted. It was the word of the Lord combined with her long-suffering patience that finally produced the miracle she so longed for.

Her story reminds me of James when he said, "Count it all joy, my brothers, when you meet trials of various kinds, for you know that the testing of your faith produces steadfastness. And let steadfastness have its full effect, that you may be perfect and complete, lacking in nothing" (1:2–4 ESV).

The one thing the Lord produced in me, after all the months of waiting on my daughter, was steadfastness, or patience. And what joy when almost a year after the accident I placed Laura's newborn brother into her arms. That was the very moment when little Laura finally woke up.

Then came the day I, with the help of a friend, packed up Laura and her purple wheelchair and her baby brother and his stroller and headed to the hospital to meet with one of her doctors for a checkup.

Upon seeing Laura's bright smile and hearing her spoken hello, this doctor, who'd sat in the council of the original twenty-six, stated, "Your daughter is not a vegetable. There's no doubt. She is awake."

A few minutes later, while my friend stood in the coffee cart line with my kids, I slipped down the hall to the hospital chapel. I found it empty, so I walked up to the front and stared at the stained-glass depiction of what appeared to be the pagan child-god of prosperity juggling vegetables. So help me, in my maturity, I shouted at that god, "Ha, ha, ha! I was right and you were wrong."

I tossed my head and turned on my heels to head back to my kids. Just as I cleared the chapel's doorway, I heard the sound of a sliding door. What? Was the chaplain's office behind a panel in the wall? I strode several steps before turning around. There stood the chaplain in the doorway, staring after me. I turned and with a bright smile waved back at her.

Her expression said it all. She couldn't deny it. My God had proved bigger than my circumstances. How glad I am that I waited on him. As it turned out, God was far more powerful than anything the doctors could pronounce. Despite my frustrations, all I needed to do to see God's faithfulness was practice a little patience.

Though Laura came back to us changed, she is still our daughter, and despite her disabilities, she continues to live at home as our beloved child. Oh, and by the way, Laura is five foot four inches tall, the same height as her mom.

Shine the Light of the Word

When we are strengthened with God's power, it's difficult to remain frustrated, as Colossians 1:11–12 explains: "We also pray that you will be strengthened with all his glorious power so you will have all the endurance and patience you need. May you be filled with joy, always thanking the Father" (NLT).

Say this simple prayer: "Open my eyes to your truth as I read Colossians 1:11–12 again."

Write down your thoughts and impressions regarding how this Scripture passage might apply to you:

_____

_____

_____

Review what you gleaned and thank God for these truths.

Yielding Prayer for the Frustrated

What if you could wipe away all your frustrations and relax in God's peace? You can, but it will take some work through prayer and yielding to the Spirit of God. These kinds of prayers can lead to the gift of peace Jesus meant for us to have all along. In fact, Jesus said in John 14:27, "I am leaving you with a gift—peace of mind and heart. And the peace I give is a gift the world cannot give. So don't be troubled or afraid" (NLT).

Shine the Light

Dear Lord,
Please turn on your light of truth over me and my frustrations. Reveal the anger, pride, or frustration that might be hiding inside me.

List the areas the Lord is revealing to you now:

_____

_____

Yield

Put your hand over your stomach and pray the following:

Dear Lord,

I yield all these things to your peace through your Holy Spirit.

With your hand still on your stomach, take deep breaths and start to relax as you repeat the prayer above until you feel God's peace drop into your spirit.

Forgive

Dear Lord,

I'm not strong enough to let go and forgive myself, you, and those who have caused me distress in any of these areas. Still, I choose to forgive. Therefore, I ask that you, through your Holy Spirit inside me, forgive all. I acknowledge that you, Lord, are without sin. Though you may have allowed these difficulties, you will use them as seeds for miracles. Thank you!

Give It All to God

Dear Lord,

I cast these frustrations at the foot of the cross. Now they are your frustrations, not mine. Thank you for setting me free from my frustrations and from trying to control my world instead of trusting you.

Pray for Healing

Dear Lord,

Please heal the pain caused by my frustrations. Thank you for your supernatural peace.

Exchange the Enemy's Work for God's Peace

Dear Lord,

Please forgive me for entertaining my frustrations. I close all the doors I have opened to the enemy in this area. In addition, I cancel any plans the enemy has for my life. I also cast out any power or influence from any evil spirits trying to frustrate me. I pray this in the power of the name and blood of Jesus.

I exchange the enemy's work for God's peace. Send the river of your peace not only to me but also to those with whom I've shared my frustrations. I pray this also in the power of the name and blood of Jesus.

Praise God—You Are Free!

Thank you, Lord! I'm free!

Pray this prayer whenever you need a redo.

5

Burdened

Finding a Way to Lighten Your Load

> Then Jesus said, "Come to me, all of you who are weary and carry heavy burdens, and I will give you rest."
>
> Matthew 11:28 NLT

I climbed up the steep mountain road alone, miles from where we'd left our 1975 red Nova sedan. I was tired, thirsty, and wondered what had happened to my young husband, Paul, as well as to our friend Gordon, who'd recently served as Paul's best man in our wedding. It had been hours since I'd last seen them.

The day had started with the thrill of adventure. The three of us, all barely adults, had driven two thousand miles straight from Texas to the base of this southern Colorado mountain range. We would have driven even farther if our sedan hadn't bottomed out on the rocks on the winding dirt road.

That's when we'd parked it and decided to hike our way into an upper valley of the Sangre de Cristo Mountains, where we planned to pitch our tents. The high valley would serve as our base camp for the next several days as we tried our hand at scaling a few of the fourteen-thousand-foot peaks that surrounded it.

At first, I enjoyed the mountain beauty, but after walking for miles beneath the burden of my backpack, I began to feel drained by the hot sun as well as the lack of oxygen at this higher altitude. Despite these difficulties, I wasn't prepared for what the man I'd married only a few months before said to me. "Linda, you're not keeping up. I think it would be better if Gordon and I ran ahead to set up camp. But don't worry. I'll come back for you soon. Okay?"

"I don't know, Paul," I said, frowning.

"I won't be gone long. I promise."

My frown deepened, and Paul gave me one of his charming smiles. "I'll even carry your backpack when I return. All right?"

Though I wasn't thrilled with their plan, I gave in, mainly because I loved the idea of my strong husband carrying my heavy burden.

I watched the guys disappear over a rise in the road as I called after them, "Don't be long, okay?"

The scenery was entertaining for a while, but the isolation that hovered in the mountain air began to feel creepy. There was not a living creature to be seen. One side of the road swept up into woody cliffs, while the other side careened into a steep drop-off, the kind that could hide a body forever. I bit my lower lip and hoped the men would return soon.

They didn't.

Hours later, I was breathing hard in the thin air as I continued my slow upward march. Suddenly, a bloodcurdling scream filled the air.

A mountain lion!

I had no doubt that the nearby cat was planning to drop off the cliffs and onto my back, tearing his fangs into my too-tall backpack stuffed with too much gear.

I wanted to run, but I was too exhausted. I only had the strength to lift my hands above my head, a trick I'd heard would make the predator think I was a larger creature. Besides, there was no place to go but up the narrowing trail, one foot after the other. So that's what I did until the shadows lengthened and blended into the enveloping darkness.

Night fell, and it had been six hours since I'd seen the guys. I was no longer sure I could go on.

I wiped at a stray tear. Why hadn't Paul returned?

I was cold and shivering when I came upon a group of rowdy men drinking brews around a campfire. I stood beyond the reach of the flickering light and wondered if it would be safe to stumble into their camp, a young woman lost, exhausted, and alone.

But the trail had ended. How could I go any farther in the darkness?

I pulled off my backpack and started to unzip it. Maybe I could pull out my sleeping bag and climb inside right where I stood. It almost seemed like a good idea, except I was hungry and thirsty and there was a mountain lion on the prowl.

Suddenly, I heard noise coming from the brush, and a flashlight beam hit my face. "Linda?"

It was Gordon!

I gasped, "Where have you two been? Where's Paul?"

Gordon lifted my backpack and began to carry it to our camp, which was located just through a tangle of trees and only a thousand or so yards from where the trail had ended. Gordon explained, "I guess this high altitude was too much for us flatlanders. Paul passed out from what must be altitude sickness, and I'm just now well enough from barfing to find you."

A few minutes later, I reunited with my sweetheart. "I'm so sorry!" he said as he tried to stand. He took only a couple of steps before he collapsed back to the ground. It seemed he was in much worse shape than I was.

However, I was glad to be found and gladder still that we'd been reunited. It took some time, but we were able to set up camp, cook freeze-dried stew on our portable stove, and sip some of the water we'd ported in before we slept in the safety of our tents.

Perhaps you know exactly how I felt the evening I was burdened and lost. Maybe you too are straining under your own heavy burden and you're wondering where God is. You want to know how to:

- find God, his help, and direction
- find relief from your heavy burdens

Find God, His Help, and Direction

One of my best moments on that long-ago evening was the moment Gordon found me in the dark.

If you're worried about being found, let me assure you that you *have* been found. It's as Psalm 46:1 says: "God is our refuge and strength, an very-present help in trouble" (KJV).

God knows right where you are, just as he knew my exact location as I hiked that winding mountain trail those many years ago. In fact, God was my constant companion that day. In between my panic, fear, and anger that the boys had left me, I shot off several earnest prayers like, "Lord, help me!" God not only heard my prayers but answered them.

Think about it. I passed only yards away from a screaming mountain lion. In Colorado, the occasional mountain lion will sometimes attack a stray hiker. Could it be that God shut this predator's mouth just as he shut the mouths of the lions in the den where Daniel spent the night (Dan. 6)?

I don't know, but I do know that not only did I survive my walk up the mountain without falling prey to either the lion or the sickness that plagued my companions, but I also found my party in the dark, only a short distance from where they had collapsed with altitude sickness.

Are you still feeling alone? Perhaps what you really need to do is realize who your traveling companion is. Romans 8:26–28 explains his presence this way:

> Meanwhile, the moment we get tired in the waiting, God's Spirit is right alongside helping us along. If we don't know how or what to pray, it doesn't matter. He does our praying in and for us, making prayer out of our wordless sighs, our aching groans. He knows us far better than we know ourselves, knows our pregnant condition, and keeps us present before God. That's why we can be so sure that every detail in our lives of love for God is worked into something good. (Message)

Let me ask you a question. How would your perception of your current struggles change if you knew for certain that

God was with you, constantly working to turn your dilemmas into good?

Good news. God *is* with you. He's at work in your circumstances now. Perhaps it's time to acknowledge God's presence and care.

> *Dear Lord,*
> *Sometimes I feel like I'm stumbling up a mountain trail in the dark as my enemies watch, waiting to pounce and devour me. Open my eyes and help me to see that you are with me and are constantly creating solutions to my dilemmas. Thank you that when I pray, "Help me," you hear me and answer. Thank you that everything is going to be all right as you work out everything for good.*
> *In Jesus's name, amen.*

Find Relief from Your Heavy Burdens

Now that we've established who your traveling companion is, I have a question. Imagine Alec Baldwin in his famous credit card commercials asking, "What's in your backpack?" What burdens are you carrying? Tap your finger next to all that apply:

- financial concerns
- job woes
- housing issues
- lack of provisions
- family dilemmas
- marriage trouble

- loved ones in crisis
- transportation difficulties
- relationship troubles
- health concerns
- not being understood
- depression, grief, or heartache
- disasters past, present, or future
- worries and fear
- stress and anxiety
- uncertain future
- _____ (fill in the blank)

Wow, I have to hand it to you. That's some list. And you've been trying to carry the weight all by yourself? No wonder you feel stressed! What you need is for someone to come along and carry your backpack for you.

Good news. Jesus said, "Come to me, all you who are weary and burdened, and I will give you rest. Take my yoke upon you and learn from me, for I am gentle and humble in heart, and you will find rest for your souls. For my yoke is easy and my burden is light" (Matt. 11:28–30).

Jesus himself wants to give us rest from our burdens. But maybe we need to read the fine print. It seems to me that Jesus is actually offering to add yet another burden onto our shoulders, the burden of his yoke. Is this some kind of divine "gotcha"?

What we have to understand is that Jesus is not offering to make our problems disappear; he's offering to give us rest for our souls while he does our heavy lifting. Otherwise, why would he say, "My yoke is easy and my burden is light"?

My friend Janet Holm McHenry explains the passage this way: "Behind the invitation is God's perfect love—his desire to meet my needs, his anticipation to bless me abundantly, and his longing to fellowship with *me*. At times, after I've laid all my praise and requests at his feet, it's as though God says to me, I will take care of all those needs—just 'Be still, and know that I am God' (Ps. 46:10)."[1]

Jesus wants to help us find rest from our burdens. We can find his rest when we simply come to him. When we recognize we are connected to his presence, we can relax in his loving care, knowing he's going to work things for the good, as Romans 8:28 says: "And we know that in all things God works for the good of those who love him, who have been called according to his purpose." If you are in Christ, meaning you've accepted his forgiveness and desire to walk with him, then you have been called to his purpose. God will work out your difficulties in answer to your prayers, or he will use your difficulties for a greater miracle. And what should you do in the meantime? Stay in his presence, trusting him with everything.

Whether or not we see (or even understand) the good that will come out of our crisis is not the point. The point is to rest in Jesus, trusting that he's moving in his own way, a way better than we could ever imagine. He's God after all, and that alone should be reason enough to let him move any way he wants. Let's talk to him about this in prayer:

Dear Lord,
   I acknowledge that you are calling me to come to you, and so here I am standing in your holy presence. I accept your yoke, which connects me more closely with you. As I allow you to put your yoke across my shoulders, I relax in

your peace. Thank you that together we will get through my difficulties and that you will lead and guide me. Your strength will get me through. Thank you!

In Jesus's name, amen.

The Story of Peace Continued

There is a way we can be free from our burdens, live into every promise of God, and win every victory through him. If you don't believe me, listen to this story of a Bible great as he might describe it.

One evening, after a late supper, I gathered my grandchildren around me and told them my story, a story I warned them never to forget. Their upturned faces glowed beneath the full moon and stars that winked over our meadow. And in that moment, I felt blessed that all of God's promises had come to pass.

I told my grandchildren, "Even as a child, I followed Moses through the desert. In fact, I was only a young man when I heard Moses tell of how God spoke to him through a burning bush. He said, 'And God told me that the promised land, the land of Canaan, was a good and large land, a land flowing with milk and honey.'"

My grandchildren giggled, partly at my imitation of Moses's gruff voice and partly because they knew well his words had proved true. So I continued, "After forty years of wandering through the desert, our people finally came to the Jordan River, the only thing that separated us from our land of promise."

I paused, looking into the eyes of each of my heirs. "You'd think our tribal leaders would have been ready to wade through this river to see this promised land for themselves. Instead, they grumbled, 'Why should we lead our flocks away from this lush grassland? If we cross this river, who knows? We might well be entering a land of war and trouble.'

"I was amazed. How could these men have such little faith? But I was equally surprised when Moses took their worries to heart. 'I'll pray about your concerns,' he told them."

I implored my wide-eyed descendants, "But what was there to pray about? Hadn't God already said the land was ours?"

The children nodded, and I continued, "After prayer, Moses was happy with the answer God had given him—to send spies, one from every tribe, into our land.

"So when twelve brave men were honored with this task, I was glad to be included. However, I was surprised that Moses charged us, 'See if the land is good and if the people are strong.'"

I stopped my story and lifted my hands toward heaven. "How could he ask such a thing of us? Moses knew that God himself had said the land was good. And if God promised this land to us, what did it matter if the people were strong? They would soon be defeated, not because of our strength but because of God's."

I continued, "The twelve of us spies spent forty days discovering that, indeed, the land was as good as God had promised. To prove it, we lugged back an abundance of pomegranates and figs as well as a cluster of grapes so heavy that it took two of us to carry it.

"But even as we journeyed back to our people, I could hear my companions complain, 'The men are giants, so tall that we could never reach them with our swords before they cut us in half.'

"'Friends,' I implored, 'if we go into the promised land with our God, why would we need to rely on our own reach to win the battle? Is the arm of God too short?'

"But they would not listen, nor would our people when they heard the complaints of the spies who whined, 'The land may be good, but compared to the inhabitants, we are like grasshoppers.'"

I folded my arms and looked at my grandchildren. "So? I ask you so?"

I stroked my gray beard and continued, "Only Joshua stood with me as I tried to calm the people. I said, 'We should go up and take possession of the land, for we can certainly do it.'

"But our leaders wept and grumbled. 'We should have stayed in Egypt,' they cried, rolling on the ground. One leader stood up and even implored the twelve of us, 'Who of you will lead us back to Egypt?'

"What was the result of their disbelief in the promise of God? God was so angry that he sent a plague that killed the ten spies who would not stand with him. Then God forbade our people from entering the land for forty years. In fact, my dear children, Joshua and I are the only ones left of that generation who are still alive."

The children looked from one to another, as they already knew that I was one of the eldest of our people.

"And when the day came for us to enter the land that God had given to our descendants, we crossed the Jordan ready for battle. Yes, there was war. But it was a battle easily won through God's strength."

I pointed to our sheep, which were bathed in the twilight's glow as they stood grazing upon the rolling hills that surrounded us. "This good land is exactly what God promised Moses."

"Grandfather," five-year-old Nun asked, "God is a faithful God?"

I nodded. "Yes, Nun. And never forget that when God makes a promise to you, he *will* keep it."

Young Jepth turned his face toward mine. "Grandfather, then God's promises are like a gift."

I smiled and pulled the child into my lap. With one hand on Jepth's head I said, "It blesses me to see one so small wiser than those foolish tribal leaders." I smiled down at my grandson. "When God makes you a promise, it is a gift. You must take hold of it and never let go. To do otherwise would be a great disrespect, a disrespect that could prompt God to give your promise to someone who will be glad to receive it" (based on Num. 13–14, 32).

You may be wondering why I told the story of Caleb, a man who carried no burden of fear or doubt either time he entered the promised land, first to spy on it, then to take it by sword.

The story is about more than Caleb and his friend Joshua. It's about the people who refused to trust God and had to carry the burden of their fear, doubt, and even defeat. Not only did they bear the weight of these difficulties, but they also died before they could see God's promises fulfilled.

How was it that Caleb, this man without the burdens of fear and doubt, was one of only two people of his generation to taste the land of milk and honey on his own parcel of the promised land?

It was because, although Caleb faced the same giants as his people, unlike them he believed God. Neither Caleb nor Joshua was afraid to go into battle because they knew they followed God into victory.

You may be thinking, *It was easy for Caleb. He had God's promise. But in my case, God hasn't promised me a thing. So of course I'm stressed and burdened. How could I be otherwise?*

Don't be so sure that you are without God's promises. Here are seven promises of God that apply to you right now:

1. You have the victory—"But thanks be to God, who gives us the victory through our Lord Jesus Christ" (1 Cor. 15:57 ESV).

2. You are forgiven through the blood of Jesus—"And the blood of Jesus, his Son, cleanses us from all sin" (1 John 1:7 NLT).

3. You have the strength of God—"I can do all things through Christ who strengthens me" (Phil. 4:13 NKJV).

4. God guides you—"In all your ways acknowledge Him, and He shall direct your paths" (Prov. 3:6 NKJV).

5. The peace of God is yours—"GOD makes his people strong. GOD gives his people peace" (Ps. 29:11 Message).

6. God provides for you—"And my God will give you everything you need because of His great riches in Christ Jesus" (Phil. 4:19 NLV).

7. You can live worry free—"Give all your worries to Him because He cares for you" (1 Pet. 5:7 NLV).

These seven promises are only a few of the thousands of promises you can find in between the covers of your

Bible. All it takes is a little digging to find the gifts God has already given you. Once you find a promise to lean on, the only thing left to do is to believe God will do what he's promised.

Yes, giants always prowl God's promised land, giants of doubt, fear, discouragement, lack, disease, and more. But you can be assured that when you believe God's promises he will empower you to slay the giants, win the victory, and enter the promised land.

Shine the Light of the Word

This business of living a burden-free life is serious business, as Hebrews 10:35–38 explains:

> Do not let this happy trust in the Lord die away, no matter what happens. Remember your reward! You need to keep on patiently doing God's will if you want him to do for you all that he has promised. His coming will not be delayed much longer. And those whose faith has made them good in God's sight must live by faith, trusting him in everything. Otherwise, if they shrink back, God will have no pleasure in them. (TLB)

Say this simple prayer: "Open my eyes to your truth as I read Hebrews 10:35–38 again."

Write down your thoughts and impressions regarding how this Scripture passage might apply to you:

_____

_____

_____

_____

Review what you gleaned and thank God for these truths.

Yielding Prayer for the Burdened

If you are ready to give God your burdens, yield to the presence of God through the following prayers.

Shine the Light

Dear Lord,

   Please turn on your light of truth over me and my burdens. Reveal to me the burdens I need to give to you.

List the burdens the Lord is revealing to you now:

_____

_____

_____

Yield

Put your hand over your stomach and pray the following:

Dear Lord,

   I yield all these heavy burdens to your peace through your Holy Spirit.

With your hand still on your stomach, take deep breaths and start to relax as you repeat the prayer above until you feel God's peace drop into your spirit.

Forgive

Dear Lord,

I'm not strong enough to let go and forgive myself, you, and those who have caused me distress in any of these areas. Still, I choose to forgive. Therefore, I ask that you, through your Holy Spirit inside me, forgive all. I acknowledge that you, Lord, are without sin. Though you may have allowed these difficulties, you will use them as seeds for miracles. Thank you!

Give It All to God

Dear Lord,

I cast these burdens at the foot of the cross. Now they are your burdens, not mine. Thank you for setting me free from straining under these burdens that now belong to you.

Pray for Healing

Dear Lord,

Please heal the pain caused by my burdens. Thank you for your supernatural peace.

Exchange the Enemy's Work for God's Peace

Dear Lord,

Please forgive me for holding on to my burdens. I close all the doors I have opened to the enemy in this area. In addition, I cancel any plans the enemy has for my life. I also cast out any power or influence from any evil spirits trying to burden me. I pray this in the power of the name and blood of Jesus.

I exchange the enemy's work for God's peace. Send the river of your peace not only to me but also to those with whom I've shared my burdens. I pray this also in the power of the name and blood of Jesus.

Praise God—You Are Free!

Thank you, Lord! I'm free!

Pray this prayer whenever you need a redo.

6

Hopeless

Finding a Light in the Dark

Why, my soul, are you downcast?
　　Why so disturbed within me?
Put your hope in God,
　　for I will yet praise him,
　　my Savior and my God.

Psalm 42:5–6

When I was five years old, I had a fluffy, white kitten named Snowball, whom I loved with all my heart. One day as I was cradling my tiny kitten in my arms, it wiggled free and ran toward the closed gate. That's when I saw them: two large dogs standing just outside my yard. I ran, screaming, "Snowball! Stop!"

But Snowball didn't stop, and just as I reached for her with my chubby fingers, she slipped beneath the bottom of the gate and into the waiting teeth of the snarling dogs.

A neighbor who heard my screams was the first on the scene, and she ran the dogs off with a stick before whisking the lifeless body of my kitten away.

This memory is one I'd like to forget, but it's one I once again encountered a few years ago at a dog obedience class with my new puppy, a miniature Labradoodle named Max.

The class was held in an old barn, and for several weeks, my classmates and I had walked our dogs through routines to sit, stay, and heel. But this day the instructor told us, "It's time to take the dogs off lead and give them some time to socialize with one another."

I was surprised by this order, but I obeyed. Still, I eyed the German shepherd and the Akita across the circle from us. These two animals had continually snapped at each other for weeks, and it had been only the owners' tugging at the dogs' leashes that had kept the dogs from tearing into one another. So I wasn't too surprised that as soon as these dogs were unleashed they turned on each other with bared fangs. As the fur flew, all the other dogs ran for their lives except for one. My little Max ran directly toward the dog fight. I barely had time to breathe a prayer as I screamed, "Max! Stop!"

But Max didn't stop.

I knew what would happen next. After all, I'd seen this scene played out once before. These two attack dogs would soon turn their fangs on my puppy, and once again that would be it.

However, Max seemed undaunted by his impending fate as he bounded toward the battling dogs. Even the dog trainer gasped as my puppy leapt toward the clash. Time melted into hopelessness, and all I could see was the terrible end that had befallen my kitten.

But instead of leaping *into* the dog fight, my bright-eyed puppy joyfully leapt *over* it. He soared over the snapping jaws, then gleefully bounded back to me.

I'm telling you this story because, like me, perhaps you've encountered situations that ended badly. Now, because of your past hurts, you're fully expecting more calamities, like getting laid off from your new job, being hurt and betrayed by friends, or never catching that much needed break. Or maybe you're in the middle of a difficulty you're certain will have no happy outcome and you're feeling the weight of your hopelessness. Let me inject a thought. Maybe things aren't as bad as they seem, especially when you consider the God factor found in Jeremiah 29:11: "'For I know the plans I have for you,' says the LORD. 'They are plans for good and not for disaster, to give you a future and a hope'" (NLT).

Wait just a minute! What's all this about a future and a hope? Isn't God going to give us the punishment we all deserve?

We are under the blood of Jesus. Our tab was paid in full by Jesus when he died on the cross for our sins. But not only did Jesus die for our sins, but he also came back to life with the resurrection power of God.

What if you were able to apply the resurrection power of God to your own circumstances? If you could do that, don't you think your hopelessness would evaporate? Let's consider this. God's resurrection power *can* be applied to your life, and when you realize this is so, you'll also realize that:

- your situation is not hopeless
- when you seek God, he will provide a way
- with God, your future is amazing

Your Situation Is Not Hopeless

Ten years ago, the sixteen-year-old daughter of my friend Julie died in a horrible accident on the freeway. Recently, I was able to sit down with Julie and talk about her loss. Julie shared that when Anna died her own grief was so relentless that she'd seriously considered suicide.

"What stopped you?" I asked.

Julie said, "I decided that despite my hopelessness and grief I would live for the sake of my son."

"Are you glad you decided to live?" I asked.

Julie nodded and opened her arms to her sweet eighteen-month-old grandson, who had toddled into the room. He climbed into her lap, and she kissed him on top of his yellow curls. Then she said, "I still miss Anna terribly. But I wouldn't trade this precious time I'm having with my grandchildren for anything."

Do you suppose that somehow Julie was able to apply God's resurrection power to her life? Yes. Not only did God help Julie find a reason to live, but he also gave her joy even in her pain.

Julie still misses Anna. Yet, she knows that one day, on the day God appoints, she and her daughter will be wondrously reunited. But until that day, Julie has work to do. She has to make a difference in the lives of her grandchildren. She has to fulfill a higher calling—to love and to be loved.

I'm sure that when the Julie of ten years ago tried to imagine her life today all she could see was hopelessness and pain. But God saw his plans for her, plans for good, plans for hope, plans he fulfilled with both his purpose and his joy.

It's the same for you. Perhaps you can't imagine surviving the hopelessness you are currently experiencing, whether it's loneliness, the death of a child, a dashed hope, a rocky marriage, a careening career, a cheating spouse, a broken dream, or something even more alarming. There's no doubt that these things are difficult. Yet, God's resurrection power can grant you hope and a future too. All you have to do is yield to his power and trust him to do the rest. Your situation is not hopeless.

> *Dear Lord,*
>
> *Sometimes when I look at what appears to be the darkness of my future, I tremble beneath the weight of hopelessness. However, you are the Lord who warned his children not to fear, you are the God who restores the hopeless, you are the God who resurrected Jesus from the dead, and you are the God who still moves in resurrection power today. So, Lord, I yield to your resurrection power in my marriage, my future, my relationships, my job, my purpose, my dreams, and, most importantly, my relationship with you. I will stand fearless before hopelessness because you are my hope. My trust is in you.*
>
> *In Jesus's name, amen.*

When You Seek God, He Will Provide a Way

The next time you face what looks like a problem that cannot be remedied, I want you to think about my puppy Max, who ran headlong into trouble that could very well have meant the end of his life, yet he was able to sail above the problem.

That's how it is when you are in relationship with God. Just when it seems as if trouble is set to destroy your hope, future, or family, God's resurrection power can help you rise above it all. But to activate God's power, we must seek God himself. It's like Charles Stanley is fond of saying, "We must remember that the shortest distance between our problems and their solutions is the distance between our knees and the floor."[1]

When you rely on God, his resurrection power will guide you out of hopelessness and into a hope-filled future.

Let's pray:

Dear Lord,
Like Linda's dog Max, teach me how to sail over my problems with joy. Teach me how to look beyond my difficulties to you. Show me how to trust you as you provide a way through my troubles in your power.
In Jesus's name, amen.

With God, Your Future Is Amazing

A friend of mine owned a condo that had been trashed by a renter. She needed to put the condo on the market, but it was in no condition to sell. When I walked through the place with her, I was appalled by all the pet hair that blew through the air vents, not to mention the nauseous smell of cat and dog urine. The carpet was black with grime and dotted with cigarette burns. The walls and stove were covered with spaghetti sauce, and the former tenant's trash was scattered throughout the unit. If this wasn't bad enough, there was a large stain on the ceiling where the upstairs toilet had overflowed. Cindy looked at me with tears in her eyes. "Who would want to buy a place like this?" she asked.

I felt my shoulders droop, and I shook my head, unsure of how to answer. This place was a hopeless mess, and I figured my friend was stuck with an unlivable unit.

How wrong I was. A couple of weeks later, after the professional cleaners and the drywall, paint, and carpet people had done their work, the condo was no longer a slum but a beautiful space. The realtor who had valued the property at well below what nearby units were selling for returned to put it on the market at a 30 percent markup.

Why the change in value? Someone had taken the time and effort to clean the place up.

This is exactly what happens when Jesus walks into our lives. Jesus changes our hearts from a slum to a palace fit for his presence.

Let's pray:

Dear Lord,
You are my majestic God, my restorer, the One in whom I trust. With your resurrection power, you bring me up from the depths of the earth. You inspire me to hope, and so I do hope. I hope in you.
In Jesus's name, amen.

The Story of Peace Continued

This biblical story tells of one man's journey from hopelessness to a life transformed by the resurrection power of God.

I was a man who could hear God's voice. I was also a man who liked to do things his own way. My stubbornness is why

I'd booked passage to Tarshish, though God had clearly directed me to go in the opposite direction, to Nineveh.

As I settled down for a nap below deck, I muttered to myself, "Nineveh! That place is certainly not for me." You see, I'd heard the stories that came out of this city of Gentiles, stories of people who were caught in a lifestyle that, well, personally disgusted me. In fact, I'd despised everyone I ever met from that place. So when God told me to go to these vermin and to tell them that God was reaching out to them, giving them a chance to set things right, I simply wasn't interested.

I settled in with the cargo as the boat set sail, smug that I would not be responsible for leading these heathen to God. Those Ninevites deserved every bit of wrath God could give them.

I must have fallen asleep, because the next thing I knew the boat was in a violent storm. The sailors woke me, insisting that I draw lots with them to see who among us had given God cause to drown us. I went along with their game of chance. So was it any surprise the lot fell to me?

The sailors looked me up and down as if I had two heads. "Who are you?" the captain bellowed above the winds.

"I am a Hebrew, and I worship the LORD, the God of heaven who made the sea and the dry land."

The men looked one to another, fear building in their eyes. "What have you done?" the captain cried, knowing full well I was on the run from the Almighty.

I let the sky answer with great flashing booms. The captain asked, "What shall we do with you to calm this storm?"

I was resigned to my hopeless fate. "Throw me overboard," I told them. But they refused. Instead, they did something

I'd so far failed to do. They turned to God. They begged him not to let them suffer for killing an innocent man.

But God and I knew I wasn't so innocent. And even when they grabbed me by the shoulders to toss me into the churning waters, my heart was still set against God. I expected death but was surprised by an open mouth of a great fish that swallowed me whole. There inside that whale, bathed in rotting fish and stomach acid with only enough putrid air to keep me alive, I experienced a living death.

I was so stubborn that it took three whole days before my heart changed, before I could tell God, "Lord, though I am losing my strength, I turn back to you. I worship you and promise to do what you ask, for you are the one who saves."

Suddenly, the fish shook with a violent spasm, and I was thrust into the surf along with the whale's vomit. I thrashed my head above the water and sucked sweet air into my lungs. The surge of the sea pushed me toward the shore, and soon my knees and palms slid into the gritty sand of the beach. The children who had been dancing in the waves went screaming for their mothers as I stood to my feet, bleached white by the whale's digestive juices and smelling like death.

It was so like God to use even my rebellion, once over-turned, as part of the message that caused the people of Nineveh to listen to my words, the words of a resurrected man.

I struggled to accept the people's reconciliation with the Almighty, as my prejudice against them ran deep. But I am now glad my mission was accomplished. It just goes to show that with God there is hope for the hopeless, including me (based on the book of Jonah).

If you are struggling with feelings of hopelessness, consider whether your feelings exist because of your own rebellion. If so, consider that God might be trying to get your attention so that you finally turn to him, finally do what you know he has called you to do. What is the last thing God told you to do? Is it something simple like loving your family or being a friend or something more complicated like forgiving someone who hurt you or performing a task or a mission that you've so far refused to do? Whatever it might be, take the first step toward God and tell him, "I turn back to you. I will do what you ask of me, but I will rely on you to help me and empower me."

If you are trying to discern God's voice and direction, relax and remember that God will never cause you to do something that goes against his Word. And know that when you say yes to God he will meet you right where you are. He will empower you and guide you to the place where you can complete the task he's called you to do.

But perhaps your feelings of hopelessness have nothing to do with rebellion against God. If you are caught up in situations beyond your control, the solution is not figuring out *how* God can save you; it's trusting that he will. As Max Lucado explains, "Trust God. No, *really* trust him. He will get you through this. Will it be easy or quick? I hope so. But it seldom is. Yet God will make good out of this mess. That's his job."[2]

Shine the Light of the Word

The secret to having a hope that never dies can be found in 1 Peter 1:3–5:

> Let us thank the God and Father of our Lord Jesus Christ. It was through His loving-kindness that we were born again

to a new life and have a hope that never dies. This hope is ours because Jesus was raised from the dead. We will receive the great things that we have been promised. They are being kept safe in heaven for us. They are pure and will not pass away. They will never be lost. You are being kept by the power of God because you put your trust in Him and you will be saved from the punishment of sin at the end of the world. (NLV)

Say this simple prayer: "Open my eyes to your truth as I read 1 Peter 1:3–5 again."

Write down your thoughts and impressions regarding how this Scripture passage might apply to you:

_____

_____

_____

_____

Review what you gleaned and thank God for these truths.

Yielding Prayer for the Hopeless

If you need to regain your hope in any area of your life, it's time to pray.

Shine the Light

Dear Lord,

Please turn on your light of truth over me and my ability to hope in you. Help me to yield any areas of hopelessness in my life to your resurrection power.

List the areas the Lord is revealing to you now:

_____

_____

_____

_____

_____

Yield

Put your hand over your stomach and pray the following:

Dear Lord,

I yield all these things to your peace as well as all of my feelings of hopelessness to you through your Holy Spirit.

With your hand still on your stomach, take deep breaths and start to relax as you repeat the prayer above until you feel God's peace drop into your spirit.

Forgive

Dear Lord,

I'm not strong enough to let go and forgive myself, you, and those who have caused me distress in any of these areas. Still, I choose to forgive. Therefore, I ask that you, through your Holy Spirit inside me, forgive all. I acknowledge that you, Lord, are without sin. Though you may have allowed these difficulties, you will use them as seeds for miracles. Thank you!

Give It All to God

Dear Lord,

I cast my hopelessness at the foot of the cross. I turn my concerns over to you. Thank you for setting me free from these concerns so I can trust you.

Pray for Healing

Dear Lord,

Please heal the pain caused by my feelings of hopelessness. Thank you for your supernatural peace.

Exchange the Enemy's Work for God's Peace

Dear Lord,

Please forgive me for giving in to hopelessness. I close all the doors I have opened to the enemy in this area. In addition, I cancel any plans the enemy has for my life. I also cast out any power or influence from any evil spirits trying to give me feelings of hopelessness. I pray this in the power of the name and blood of Jesus.

I exchange the enemy's work for God's peace. Send the river of your peace not only to me but also to those with whom I've shared my hopelessness. I pray this also in the power of the name and blood of Jesus.

Praise God—You Are Free!

Thank you, Lord! I'm free!

Pray this prayer whenever you need a redo.

7

Offended

Finding Relief from Hard Feelings

> But now is the time to get rid of anger, rage, malicious behavior, slander, and dirty language.
>
> Colossians 3:8 NLT

Many summers ago, I, along with two thousand other speakers, attended a National Speakers Association convention in Dallas, Texas. I have to admit, I was mesmerized by our incoming president Naomi Rhode—a charming woman who used the platform to do what she does best: exude the love of God.

Naomi shared the platform with a hilarious comedian by the name of Dale Irvin. He would lie in wait until a break in the program, then spring to the microphone to give one of his sidesplitting "reports," a rousing parody of the speakers' messages.

The crowd howled with laughter and stomped their feet at Dale's comedic spin. But the speaker who became the brunt of many of Dale's jokes was dear Naomi, who handled Dale's jabs with grace and good humor.

Then came the evening when those who'd been so thoroughly roasted by Dale got to take the stage to roast him back. When Naomi walked across the platform in her sparkling silver gown, the audience members held their breath. How would she respond now that she had control of a microphone aimed directly at Dale?

She started by telling of her recent visit to Broadway to see *Les Misérables*, a musical set in postrevolutionary France. She told how Jean Valjean stole a loaf of bread to feed his family, then paid for the crime with nineteen years of hard labor.

Upon being paroled, Valjean faced rejection and hunger until he happened upon the home of the bishop of Digne, the only person to show Valjean compassion. The bishop invited Valjean to his supper table to give him a message of hope before giving him a warm bed for the night. But that evening, Jean Valjean did the unthinkable. He stole the bishop's silverware and slipped into the night.

He was soon captured by the police and thrown at the bishop's feet. But instead of condemning Valjean, the bishop extended grace and even agreed with Valjean's claim that he'd been given the silverware. Then the bishop did something unexpected. He reached for the silver candlesticks still sitting on his table and told Valjean, "But, my friend, you left so early you forgot I gave these also. Would you leave the best behind?"

Naomi said, "The bishop's motive? He wanted Valjean to know what it meant to receive grace."

Naomi called Dale to the platform and then presented him with a beautifully wrapped package. Dale opened it to reveal a pair of silver candlesticks.

The crowd was amazed that Naomi, instead of responding with barbs, had extended Dale grace. What a moment—a moment that left this quick-witted comedian completely speechless.

I recently caught up with Naomi, and she talked about the incident with these wise words: "I can choose to be offended or not. So when it came to Dale's parodies of me, I chose not to personalize his words or to let them offend me." She chuckled. "In fact, Dale's barbs toward me became a well-recognized association joke."

I also spoke with Dale about his exchanges with Naomi, and he explained that his comedy is never meant to offend but to commend. He added, "I say nothing mean and mean only to be entertaining."

My hat is off to both Naomi and Dale, and their examples lead me to ask you, "How often do you choose to take offense at things that were never meant to offend?"

Perhaps, if you're like me, you'll want to resolve to do a better job at extending grace to those whose remarks unintentionally upset you.

Still, you might be wondering, *What about those jabs that were meant to sting me? What do I do with those?*

Once again, you have the power to choose whether or not to be offended. If an offense has already taken root, you still have the power to make a choice, the choice to forgive.

Silver-candlestick living is based on Proverbs 19:11, which says, "Sensible people control their temper; they earn respect by overlooking wrongs" (NLT). Consider also the wise words of my friend Joy Schneider, who believes it's possible to find some benefit in offense. As she explains, "Opportunity lurks at the door of offense." In other words, if you can look past an offense, you may find an opportunity to make a friend, build a bond, share a goal or a cause, retrieve information you need, learn a lesson, lend or receive a helping hand, laugh at yourself, or have a happier day.

If you're not sure if this is true, check it out for yourself. The next time you feel the sting of offense, instead of snapping, pouting, or even counting to ten, say a quick prayer like, "God, what are you trying to show me? What opportunity is hiding here?"

When I take the time to do this, I often discover amazing opportunities I might have easily missed, including a ministry connection, a sweet friendship, or a healing discussion.

That's all well and good, you might be thinking, *but what about the times when offenses are so serious that they can't be overlooked and I'm left to deal with bitterness and rage? What then?*

I'd say it's time to seek the power of God so that you can supernaturally forgive the offender, not because they deserve it but because you deserve to walk free and clear of the pain and trauma of the hurt you've been trying to live with.

But watch out! When it comes to the business of forgiveness, there are pitfalls to avoid. It's as author Pam Farrel once said:

> There is a lot of confusion over forgiveness. We all know we should do it. But we're not sure what "it" looks like. . . . People think forgiveness is sweeping the offense under the rug with the phrase, "Let's just not talk about it," and pretend it never happened. That isn't forgiveness; that's denial.

Sometimes we don't forgive because we think forgiveness means we must reconcile. But forgiveness and reconciliation are actually two separate acts. Forgiveness is a vertical act, a private prayer that takes place between you and God in response to a person's actions. Reconciliation is a horizontal act that involves forgiveness on the part of the person who was offended and true repentance by the person who did the harm. It is extremely difficult and unwise to reconcile unless you have first experienced the vertical act of forgiveness with God.[1]

In other words, when an offense cannot be overlooked because it's too serious to brush aside or too dangerous to ignore or deny, you can still deal with it through a vertical conversation with God like the following:

Dear Lord,

You know what _____ did, and it's not something I can overlook or pretend never happened. Please give me wisdom on how to respond because I want to be free from my pain and bitterness. Therefore, I'm doing the only thing I can. I'm giving this offense to you. Please do not count this offense as sin against my offender but shine your truth over their heart and mind as you bring them to repentance. But even if repentance never happens, I am still willing to let go through your power. I am also giving you my trauma and asking you to heal me of my pain.

In Jesus's name, amen.

After praying such a prayer, you may still want to ask God to guide you into reconciliation, for as Matthew 5:23–24 says,

"If you take your gift to the altar and remember your brother has something against you, leave your gift on the altar. Go and make right what is wrong between you and him. Then come back and give your gift" (NLV).

Just note that reconciliation may not come easily, quickly, or even at all if the other party does not want to repent for their part in the difficulty. Still, why not start the reconciliation process and pray:

> *Dear Lord,*
>
> *I ask that in your perfect timing you will give me the opportunity to miraculously reconcile with _____. Shine the light of your truth in this matter so that misunderstandings can come to light and repentance can be achieved, even if it turns out that I am the one who needs to apologize. If I need to repent, show me, and show me how. If through my repentance you call me to reconcile, go before me and with me and give me the words to speak to the one I offended.*
>
> *Help me not to miss an opportunity of reconciliation if and when it should come. In the meantime, help my heart to be free of bitterness so that I may enjoy your peace that passes understanding.*
>
> *In Jesus's name, amen.*

As you continue to learn how to work through offenses, let me offer you some tips that will help you:

- live in supernatural love
- learn how to let go
- draw closer to God

Live in Supernatural Love

When it comes down to it, living a silver-candlestick life means that we must live a life filled with supernatural love. This is the kind of love described in 1 Corinthians 13:4–7:

> Love is patient and kind. Love is not jealous or boastful or proud or rude. It does not demand its own way. It is not irritable, and it keeps no record of being wronged. It does not rejoice about injustice but rejoices whenever the truth wins out. Love never gives up, never loses faith, is always hopeful, and endures through every circumstance. (NLT)

Evangelist Bill Bright once said of this passage:

> As you read those words, you might think, *This describes an impossible love. I could never live up to such a standard.*
>
> And you would be correct. Who is able to love like that? That is why our only hope is to cast ourselves completely upon Him and invite the Holy Spirit to fill and empower us to love in a supernatural way. In humble faith, we will be filled with a love that is far above the natural, worldly variety. It will be a love against which the world can have no defense, for it confounds all expectations. It will overcome any barrier.
>
> Through such a love as this, God will accomplish supernatural goals through you. And believe it or not, you can love anyone in this way—by faith.[2]

If you need to tap into the kind of faith that will lead to supernatural love, try praying:

Dear Lord,
I have a few people in my life I'm having trouble loving, including _____. *Please empower me with your*

Holy Spirit to help me become aware of the supernatural love you're constantly giving me in an endless supply. Then shine this love through me on to those I've been unable to love in my human strength. I ask that you give me your compassionate perspective as well as your ability to love the difficult.

In Jesus's name, amen.

Learn How to Let Go

Hebrews 12:15 says, "Look after each other so that none of you fails to receive the grace of God. Watch out that no poisonous root of bitterness grows up to trouble you, corrupting many" (NLT). When we read such passages, we know that our God calling is not to become angry, bitter people. But that said, how do we let go of offenses?

I recently found myself struggling with this very issue as I waited with a group of friends at an airport. One of my friends seemed to purposely turn her back to me, blocking me from joining in the conversation. After forty-five minutes of trying to break through the wall, I felt shunned, angry, and hurt. Later, back in Colorado, I went to bed with the sting of the shunning on my heart. The next morning, I told the Lord, "I am trying to let go of this offense, but it still hurts."

He whispered to my heart, "Give the pain to me."

So I prayed, "Here you go, Lord," but it was to no effect.

The Lord told me, "You need to let go."

"I'm trying."

"Then quit trying and let go. It's as simple as that."

In my mind's eye, I saw myself holding a beach ball. The Lord coaxed, "If you are 'trying' to let go, you are still holding on. Just let go."

I saw my hands open so that the ball fell to the ground. Then, in my spirit, I dropped the offense, just as I'd dropped that ball. I felt God's sweet presence. I felt refreshed as if a shower had washed away yesterday's grime. The Lord spoke to me again. "You do not need to go into today wearing yesterday's dirt. You have the power to let go and to come to me so you can be clean."

Without the offense in my heart, I was soon able to re-engage my friend in a meaningful way. I never cornered her and demanded an apology or an explanation for her behavior because I no longer needed one. Today is a new day, a day to enjoy the blessing of the friends God has placed in my life, a day to brush aside yesterday's offenses and move forward in love.

Perhaps you are rolling your eyes at my illustration, saying under your breath, "Linda, the offense you let go of is petty compared to what I'm struggling with."

Even so, the process of letting go is the same. If you are ready to be free from your pain, pray:

Dear Lord,

I've had a difficult time letting go of certain offenses, including _____. Help me to see that in my trying I was only clinging to the very thing that offended me. Give me the power and the strength to let go.

I declare that I am letting go. I am dropping the offense. It's falling from my grasp. It's gone. This is the end of my pain and the beginning of peace. I am refreshed and clean before you. Thank you, Lord!

In Jesus's name, amen.

Draw Closer to God

Do you think it's any accident that Jesus said, "Bless those who curse you. Pray for those who hurt you" (Luke 6:28 NLT)?

Neither do I, for there is a blessing in living a silver-candlestick life. In fact, author Karol Ladd writes, "When we begin to pray for our enemies, our hearts begin to change. Anger subsides as we begin to give our hurts to the Father and sincerely pray for those who hurt us. I want to encourage you to try it and then watch what God begins to do in your heart."[3]

I absolutely agree with Ladd. Praying for our enemies and pushing beyond the offenses we encounter will change our hearts and, most importantly, draw us closer to God.

Let's pray:

Dear Lord,

Please bless my enemies and help those who have hurt me, including _____. I also ask that you would draw us closer still to you. I praise you for your great love and forgiveness, not only for me but also for those who have offended me. I pray that the truth will set us all free in forgiveness, love, and reconciliation.

In Jesus's name, amen.

The Story of Peace Continued

If you're curious to see the power of forgiveness, read my take on what happened to a man who was forgiven of more than most of us could ever imagine.

My friends guided me as I stumbled into the inn. Though the day was bright, all I could see was the whiteness that had suddenly blinded me. I was not a man struck by lightning but a man who'd struck the ground when a heavenly being had blocked my way and called me by name. "Saul! Saul! Why are you persecuting me?"

As I'd lain on the ground, I'd choked with both dust and fear. Still, I managed to stammer, "Who are you, Lord?"

"I am Jesus, the one you are persecuting!"

It couldn't be.

Only days ago, I had held the coats of those who had gathered the rocks and stoned Stephen to death. As Stephen's blood had splattered, he'd lifted his face toward the sky and called out, "Look, I see the heavens open and the Son of Man standing in the place of honor at God's right hand!"

I had felt rage at his words of blasphemy, the same rage that had given those who threw the stones energy to hasten the man's ghastly death. It was a death that had ignited my thirst for the blood of all followers of this Christ. It was in fact the very reason I'd hurried down the road to Damascus with papers giving me the authority to arrest any Christ followers I found there. And then this Jesus, this one I'd presumed to be rotting in his grave, had stood before me.

I had lain frozen in fear as Jesus, in his risen glory, had said, "Now get up and go into the city, and you will be told what you must do." My friends had seen the flash and heard the sound of a voice, but they had seen no one except me lying face down in the road.

Long after my companions left me in a room at the inn, I lay in my bed, blind, with my face turned to the wall. The innkeeper's wife could not coax me to eat her bread or taste her drink. Instead, I lay on my pallet trembling, knowing that I who had thought myself a defender of God was in fact one of his worst enemies.

What would he do to me for persecuting him? My only solace was Stephen's last words regarding those who stoned him. "Lord, don't charge them with this sin!"

After three days of terror, tears, and repentance, I had a vision. I saw a man named Ananias come into my room to lay hands on me so that my eyes were healed. So when I heard voices in the courtyard, I turned from my wall to listen.

A woman pleaded, "You mustn't go in. Can't you see it's a trap?"

A man answered, "But God said . . ."

"But would God have you walk into your death? You know this man is here to arrest you and to lead you to the same death that our brother Stephen suffered. Ananias, this is folly!"

"You must hear me, my dear wife. God said, 'Go.'"

I heard footsteps, followed by the sound of the curtain to my room sliding open. I sat up and stammered, "Ananias? Your name is Ananias?"

The man might have nodded. I don't know. But I do know he put his rough hand on my head and began to pray. "Lord, it is your good pleasure to heal this man and to open his blind eyes, so in obedience, I am asking that it be so. In the mighty name of Jesus."

As the scales that had blinded me fell away, I saw him, the man who had dared to face his own death for the sake of obeying the Lord Jesus.

He gave me a smile and patted my shoulder, but I was impressed by his courage to push past any fear or offense I had caused him. He would be my inspiration to say yes to Jesus, no matter what he might ask of me. And like Ananias, I would prove to be a man of my word. How grateful I am that first Stephen, then Ananias, through the mighty power of Jesus himself, had forgiven me so that I could share this good news of God's forgiveness with the world (based on Acts 7:51–8:1; 9:1–19).

Saul became the apostle Paul, the man who wrote thirteen books of the New Testament. Besides Jesus Christ, he's considered the most important figure of the early church.

Saul was on a mission to snuff out those who followed Jesus, but God was on a mission to lead Saul to become not only a Christ follower but also one of the most influential evangelists who ever lived.

But just think, if Ananias had refused to forgive the offense of a man who had come to town to take him and his loved ones to their execution, our world would not know Paul or his writings.

Ananias probably did not know how influential Paul would become to the body of Christ. So why did he accept God's call to minister to this man who had sworn himself his enemy? Though Ananias may not have liked the idea of going to his enemy to pray for him, he did it because God told him to go. It was as simple as that.

So if you are holding back, determined to keep a pet offense all to yourself, consider this. God is also telling you to go! So go and obey him. Go and forgive. And if need be, go and apologize and offer to reconcile. You'll never know what miracle may be waiting at the door of your offense unless you push through it.

Shine the Light of the Word

Jesus gave us clear instruction on how to handle offenses in Luke 6:27–31 when he said:

I say to you who hear Me, love those who work against you. Do good to those who hate you. Respect and give thanks for those who try to bring bad to you. Pray for those who make it very hard for you. Whoever hits you on one side of the face, turn so he can hit the other side also. Whoever takes your coat, give him your shirt also. Give to any person who asks you for something. If a person takes something from you, do not ask for it back. Do for other people what you would like to have them do for you. (NLV)

Say this simple prayer: "Open my eyes to your truth as I read Luke 6:27–31 again."

Write down your thoughts and impressions regarding how this Scripture passage might apply to you:

_____

_____

_____

Review what you gleaned and thank God for these truths.

Yielding Prayer for the Offended

If you need to regain your freedom in this area of your life, it's time to pray.

Shine the Light

Dear Lord,
   Please turn on your light of truth over me and my ability to sidestep offenses, bitterness, and unforgiveness. Help me to yield all my past and present offenses to you.

List the areas the Lord is revealing to you now:

_____

_____

_____

_____

_____

Yield

Put your hand over your stomach and pray the following:

Dear Lord,

I yield all these offenses as well as my feelings of bitterness to your peace through your Holy Spirit.

With your hand still on your stomach, take deep breaths and start to relax as you repeat the prayer above until you feel God's peace drop into your spirit.

Forgive

Dear Lord,

I'm not strong enough to let go and forgive myself, you, and those who have caused me distress in any of these areas. Still, I choose to forgive. Therefore, I ask that you, through your Holy Spirit inside me, forgive all. I acknowledge that you, Lord, are without sin. Though you may have allowed these difficulties, you will use them as seeds for miracles. Thank you!

Give It All to God

Dear Lord,

I cast my offenses at the foot of the cross. Now they belong to you, not me. I know you will set free not only my offenders but me as well. Thank you that I can walk in your freedom.

Pray for Healing

Dear Lord,

Please heal the pain caused by my feelings of being offended. Thank you for your supernatural peace.

Exchange the Enemy's Work for God's Peace

Dear Lord,

Please forgive me for entertaining offenses. I close all the doors I have opened to the enemy in this area. In addition, I cancel any plans the enemy has for me. I also cast out any power or influence from any evil spirits of rage, offense, and bitterness coming against me. I pray this in the power of the name and blood of Jesus.

I exchange the enemy's work for God's peace. Send the river of your peace not only to me but also to those with whom I've shared offense. I pray this also in the power of the name and blood of Jesus.

Praise God—You Are Free!

Thank you, Lord! I'm free!

Pray this prayer whenever you need a redo.

8

Anxious

Finding God's Bliss

> For God has not given us a spirit of fear, but
> of power and of love and of a sound mind.
>
> 2 Timothy 1:7 NKJV

Perhaps you sometimes feel like Indiana Jones in the 1981 movie *Raiders of the Lost Ark*. In this fast-paced adventure set in 1939, Indiana is an archaeologist looking to find the lost ark of the covenant before the Nazis do. But on his quest, Indy has to face his worst fear as he and his friend Sallah look down into the dark, ancient ruins of the Well of Souls. Sallah asks, "Indy, why does the floor move?"

Indy grabs Sallah's torch and drops it onto the floor several feet below. The glow illuminates a pit of slithering vipers, and Indy flinches. "Snakes. Why'd it have to be snakes?"

Sallah's response includes a line that I like to tell God whenever I'm bringing him what appears to be a fearful situation: "You go first." God does go before us, as Psalm 59:10 explains: "My God on whom I can rely. God will go before me." But still, even knowing that God will go into difficulties with us doesn't mean that fear can't sneak up on us, as it did to me when I was a nineteen-year-old college student at the Glorieta conference center in New Mexico.

I awoke at dawn and decided to take an early morning walk in the beautiful prayer garden. While walking up the wide stone stairs next to a cascading fountain, I happened to notice something coiled just inches beneath my uplifted sandaled foot—a foot poised to step on that location in the next second. I froze and stared down at the now rattling diamondback snake beneath me. With my foot still held aloft, I jumped backward, just out of striking distance. I watched as the rattler uncoiled itself and slithered into a crevice under one of the stones.

I scurried back down to the base of the fountain, where I met up with a group of my friends. "Be careful," I told them as I pointed up the hill. "I just saw a rattler!"

My friends took this news in stride. In fact, one of the girls handed me her camera. "Linda, could you take a picture of us by the fountain?"

"Sure," I said as they posed. Trouble was, I had to crouch low to get everyone in the shot. Just as my finger started to snap the picture, one of the boys said, "Hey, Linda, is that a rattlesnake behind you?"

My finger clicked the picture as I screamed and leapt straight into the air.

The boy grinned, and I realized I was a victim of a practical joke. Though there wasn't a second rattler, I did get a nice shot of my friends' expressive reactions to my unbridled fear.

But consider this. There are thirty-seven hundred species of snakes in the world, and approximately eight thousand people are bitten annually by venomous varieties, which results in fifteen fatalities.[1] With so much slithering danger, shouldn't we all just stay home?

But are you safe from snakes at home? I'm wondering because I once saw a garden snake slither into my house through an open door in our mud room, a room piled with supplies for my daughter's care. Trouble is, I never found where that snake went. So what should I do? Wear tall rubber boots in the house in case a snake is hiding beneath my couch?

I'm laughing at this thought because in the ten years that have passed since this snake-on-the-loose incident I've never found any signs of that snake, which probably slithered back outside. (I left the door open so it would.) Besides, I think the raccoon that used to get in through the dog door would have eaten it by now. Now I shut the dog door at night, and I don't worry about that snake. I long ago decided this concern is just another opportunity to trust God, snake or no snake.

If my snake stories left you feeling a little queasy, I hope that I'll soon convince you to attempt to live a fearless life, regardless of the kinds of snakes (two-legged or not) you might encounter.

Yes, there may be snakes, but so what? Jesus said in Luke 10:19, "I have given you authority to trample on snakes and scorpions and to overcome all the power of the enemy; nothing will harm you." If we have that kind of power over snakes and other hostilities, why should we be afraid?

The answer is simple. We fear because we are human. But the trouble is that when we give in to fear it will stop us from having the courage to say yes to God. Max Lucado says:

When fear shapes our lives, safety becomes our god. When safety becomes our god, we worship the risk-free life. Can the safety lover do anything great? Can the risk-adverse accomplish noble deeds? for God? for others? No.

The fear-filled cannot love deeply. Love is risky.

They cannot give to the poor. Benevolence has no guarantee of return.

The fear-filled cannot dream wildly. What if their dreams sputter and fall from the sky?

The worship of safety emasculates greatness. No wonder Jesus waged a war against fear.[2]

Lucado's remark reveals a great truth. We cannot live a full life in Christ when we let fear—instead of God and his great love—rule our hearts.

So what will help us break free from anxiety? We need to join the war Jesus waged against fear and its twin sister, worry. If you want to trade your anxiety for God's bliss, you will need to learn how to:

- break the stronghold of fear
- break the stronghold of worry

Break the Stronghold of Fear

Author Neil Anderson explains the fear stronghold this way:

Fear is a thief. It erodes our faith, plunders our hope, steals our freedom, and takes away our joy of living the abundant life in Christ. Phobias are like the coils of a snake—the more we give into them, the tighter they squeeze. Tired of fighting, we succumb to the temptation and surrender to our fears. But what seems like an easy way out becomes, in reality, a prison of unbelief—a fortress of fear that holds us captive.[3]

The Bible tells us many times not to fear with admonitions such as "Do not be afraid" and "Fear not." But even though Jesus himself told us to "fear not," he did make what sounds like a contradictory statement when he said, "Dear friends, don't be afraid of those who want to kill your body; they cannot do any more to you after that. But I'll tell you whom to fear. Fear God, who has the power to kill you and then throw you into hell. Yes, he's the one to fear" (Luke 12:4–5 NLT).

I respond to Jesus by saying, "When you put it that way, I want to tremble and then to thank you for rescuing me from such a terrible fate through your death and resurrection!"

But to you, dear reader, I respond by saying that we are not to be afraid of the devil, for the real power to destroy comes from God himself, who is indeed awesome and mighty. However, you were designed to trust Jesus, not only with your present difficulties but also with your hereafter.

I believe God wanted me to be sure to drive this point home, as my reading today in *Jesus Calling* said, "I want you to know how safe and secure you are in My Presence. That is a fact, totally independent of your feelings. You are on your way to heaven; nothing can prevent you from reaching that destination."[4]

We who are under the blood of Christ have a blessed assurance that we belong to him, and being aware of his love for us is actually the key to banishing fear. First John 4:18 reminds us, "There is no fear in love. Perfect love puts fear out of our hearts. People have fear when they are afraid of being punished. The man who is afraid does not have perfect love" (NLV).

But when we lose our focus through distraction or rebellion, fear can slither into our lives. Sue Falcone, in her devotional for women, says, "Fear always comes when we leave God out of our lives. Throughout my life I can look back at the times when I lived in the most fear. My pattern shows I was running from God, thinking I could handle my life."[5]

Don't pull a Jonah and run away from the fear God is calling you to face. Remember who is going into the fearful situation with you: the Lord of the universe, the God who loves you, who will give you strength, and who will see you safely through in his peace. Psalm 29:11 puts it this way: "The LORD gives strength to his people; the LORD blesses his people with peace."

Still, I have a warning for you. Beware of the fear the enemy uses to sabotage your walk with God. The enemy tries to stir up fear in your life through false reports or imaginations, and it can hit you when the enemy would like nothing more than to distract you from deepening your relationship with God or what God has called you to do.

Consider what happened to me today as I set to work on this chapter. Because I had some catching up to do on my writing, I decided to stay home to write while my husband and his friends set out for the Triple Bypass, a 120-mile bicycle ride in the Colorado high country from Evergreen to Avon. This ride is a true test of strength because it encompasses several mountain passes and a gain of over ten thousand feet in elevation.

I was worried about this year's ride because it coincided with monsoon conditions, so before my hubby left for the starting line, I blessed him to have a great and, of course, safe ride.

Periodically, I checked on Paul's progress with an app on my smartphone that showed me his location by the minute. Later that afternoon, when I stopped for my coffee break, I wondered how the men were faring with the rain-slicked mountain passes. This time when I checked Paul's location, the app showed he was in a hospital.

I suddenly felt fear as I thought of all the things that could have gone wrong—a dive over a mountain edge, an accident, exhaustion, or even a heart problem. With a shaking finger, I dialed Paul's number and was relieved when he picked up. "So what happened?" I asked.

"What do you mean?"

"Were you or Mitch hurt? Why are you at the hospital?"

"What are you talking about?"

"The satellite shows you're smack in the middle of the hospital in Frisco!"

Paul laughed. "We're actually a mile away, eating sandwiches. We're all fine and having a great ride."

What a relief. It seems I'd been misled by a satellite beam bouncing off a low-hanging cloud.

So no matter the report you get, check in with God, just as I checked in with Paul. "Lord, did you hear that? Is it true? How do you want me to respond? Will you walk with me through this?"

The answer is yes he will. What the enemy uses to distract you from God's presence or purpose God uses to keep you closer to him than ever.

With Jesus's help, we can wage war against fear. Let's pray:

Dear Lord,

I am so relieved that I can trust in you, no matter what is going on in my life or in the world. It's like Psalm 56:3–4 says: "When I am afraid, I put my trust in you. In God, whose word I praise—in God I trust and am not afraid. What can mere mortals do to me?"

Lord, help me to stay aware of your presence and to turn to you in every situation I face, for you go into my difficulties before me, and you turn my troubles into stepping-stones of miracles. Therefore, I give my fear to you and exchange it for the recognition of your love and faithfulness.

In Jesus's name, amen.

Break the Stronghold of Worry

Worry is the twin sister of fear, and a lot of the fear-defeating principles described above also apply to worry.

What benefit does worry provide? It's like Jesus explained in Luke 12:25–26: "Who of you by worrying can add a single hour to your life? Since you cannot do this very little thing, why do you worry about the rest?"

It's not that there aren't plenty of things to worry about. But most of the things we spend our time worrying about never happen. For example, despite the fact that I've disturbed several venomous snakes in my lifetime, I've never been bitten. So would it be wise for me to worry myself sick about being bitten by a poisonous snake when I walk outside to check the mail? Well, no, especially when you consider the statistics on snakebites I cited earlier. Despite the fact that there are seven billion people on the planet, only fifteen will die from a snakebite this year, which makes for pretty low odds that I will die from a biting viper on the way to retrieve a bill.

Of course, I'm not advocating pitching a tent in a venomous snake pit, but I am giving you permission to enjoy your patio and to leave your fear of grass snakes behind, which of course aren't venomous anyway.

Worrying about snakes or other troubling things is a waste of time. Still, worry is a hard habit to break, and we may find ourselves in need of divine help if we want to be free from it. I recently underlined my *Dear Jesus* devotional when it addressed this very topic. "Beloved, you do need my help, because trying to fight this battle on your own has been so counterproductive. Now you're worrying about worrying! Your best strategy is to stop focusing on this problem and to put your energy into communicating more with me."[6]

That said, I think it's time to pray:

Dear Lord,

I've racked up quite a list of worries that I'd like to now present to you. My worry cannot change the outcome of any concern. But you can! Therefore, I want to talk to you about my worries and to ask that you orchestrate the outcomes for your purposes and my good. I ask that your healing and miraculous touch would be over _____
and that your presence in these circumstances would make all the difference. Now my worries belong to you. Thank you, Lord!

In Jesus's name, amen.

The Story of Peace Continued

Remember when I advised against pitching your tent on a viper pit? Well, sometimes, despite our best intentions, we end up in the very place we tried to avoid, leaving us to ask, like the Bible character below, "Why'd it have to be snakes?"

What can I say? I may have been the first to grumble against God and Moses. I was having a bad day, and I was tired of the sand and the traveling, always the sand. We'd walked from the Red Sea to the promised land and now back to the Red Sea because we were serving another forty years in the desert because our tribes had refused to take the land God had promised us. We were walking, pitching camp, and then walking some more. In the past few weeks, our nation had been attacked, some of us even kidnapped.

Now we had to skirt the wilderness shortcuts because the kingdoms of the desert refused to let us pass through their lands, terrified that what we'd done to the city of Hormah we'd also do to them. So on this day, a day I felt such deep discouragement, I blurted to my friend Amaras, "What was God thinking when he told Moses to bring us out of Egypt? Was it so we could die in the desert? There is no bread! There is no water! And I detest this miserable sand!"

Amaras agreed with my feelings and even repeated my complaints to her husband. The words I'd muttered to a friend were soon the talk of our nation, as one voice after another joined with mine. The clamor of our complaints rose to God's ears.

That night my husband, Seth, and I tried to set up camp. I'd busied myself with unpacking the tent when the screams started. I lifted the flap and peered out just as Amaras, who'd also been making camp, joined her screams with the others.

It was past sunset, but there was still enough light to see that my friend had a red viper attached to her arm. Her husband grabbed it by its tail and snapped its head against a nearby rock. But Amaras had two large puncture wounds on her arm. I ran to her, and as I did, the ground began to slither. Scales slid upon scales, creating a sort of sizzling that grew louder by the moment. The screams of our tribes continued to build, but I fell quiet. I stood spellbound, staring into a pair of yellow eyes. The snake before me lifted its head, then without warning the creature flung itself through the air in an upward motion. As my screams joined the others, the snake's fangs sunk deep into my thigh.

My screams continued as the pain of the viper's fiery poison began to flow into me. I watched as Amaras fell to one knee. "No!" I yelled, watching as another sidewinder lunged at her. Her husband pulled her from its reach just in time, then carried her to their tent. But her tent was as perilous as mine, as the scaly creatures slithered around us in the night. My husband, Seth, kept his sword ready, slamming his blade on the snakes that slithered into our abode. As for me, I knew I was slowly dying. First, my flesh began to rot away from the fang marks as my belly began to cramp. Then I started to bleed from my nose. By dawn, the snakes had for the most part slithered back into their holes and crevices, so I stumbled back to Amaras's tent. "How is she?" I asked Gabor, who was cradling his wife in his arms. He looked up at me with tears mixed with blood. "I couldn't keep the snakes away from her. She's gone."

I put my hand to my mouth and watched as he stroked her head with his own snakebit hand. I turned to find Seth standing beside me. I told him, "You must go to the tribal council and beseech them to ask Moses to pray for us."

As evening drew near, my husband came with Moses's answer. God had instructed Moses to make a bronze snake and to put it up on a pole. Seth told me, "Anyone who is bitten and can look at it will live."

I clasped my hands. "How soon before it's ready?"

"Moses began his work early this day, so maybe in the morning."

"If I should live that long," I said as Seth helped me back to the tent. I was glad that my daughters, their husbands, and their little ones had survived the night. I knew because their tent was close and my grandchildren had checked on me throughout the day. So as the clouds began to turn into dark shades of gold, I was surprised when little Talia, my five-year-old granddaughter, came running into my tent. "Grandmother, I have been praying for you," she said.

"You should be at home now. The snakes could appear at any time."

I watched as Talia turned to run the way she'd come. She made it a few steps before a viper lunged, striking her arm. She screamed and tried to shake it off as Seth ran to her. He knocked the snake away before carrying her back to our tent.

I didn't mind death for me, as I'd accepted my fate. But I did not accept it for Talia. She was too young, too innocent to pay for the sins of our tribe.

I spent the night holding her in my arms as I wept, watching as Seth sliced the heads off the vipers that tried to enter our tent. Somehow I must have dozed and was surprised to see the dawn. I looked down at my granddaughter. Talia was now so very pale. Blood dripped from her eyes and streaked down her cheeks. "I'm dying, Grandmother," she solemnly whispered.

I wiped the blood from my mouth and kissed her cheek, knowing that we would die together.

Suddenly, a trumpet sounded in the camp. Seth pushed the flap to our tent open. "Dawn is here," he said. "The snakes are gone. It's safe to come out."

He carried Talia in one of his strong arms and helped support me with the other as I followed our neighbors. The healthy ones buzzed with the names of those who had died in the night, while the sick, including Gabor, stumbled with the crowd to the tabernacle.

There stood Moses, who said, "God sent this plague of fiery snakes because you grumbled against him and against me. But I have prayed for you and followed God's command to make a bronze snake on a pole. God says that anyone who has been bitten who looks at this snake will live."

I let my eyes follow the crook of Moses's finger, then gaze upon the bronze snake. Immediately, I felt life begin to surge back into my body. I turned to Seth. "Can you get Talia to open her eyes?"

He shook his head. "You try," he said as he handed me Talia's limp body.

Fear flowed through my being as I coaxed, "Talia, my sweet child, open your eyes. Look, look at the pole."

Talia's eyes cracked, and I pointed at the bronze snake. "Look at the snake," I encouraged.

Her eyes were opening wider now. "I see it," she whispered as she lifted her head. Color returned to her cheeks. "I see it, Grandmother."

I hugged her neck and said, "Because of God's mercy, we will both live" (based on Num. 21:1–9).

Jesus talked about this story in John 3:14 when he said, "Just as Moses lifted up the snake in the wilderness, so the Son of Man must be lifted up." Jesus was referring to himself. Jesus became the snake on the pole when he died on the cross. Because we've all been snake bit with the poison of sin, we all need to look to Jesus for the forgiveness of our sins. Looking to Jesus is the same cure for our worries and fears. When we look to Jesus, instead of concentrating on our worries and fears, Jesus will give us his peace as they fade away.

Shine the Light of the Word

The cure for anxiety can be found in Jesus's words, "Peace I leave with you; my peace I give you. I do not give to you as the world gives. Do not let your hearts be troubled and do not be afraid" (John 14:27).

Say this simple prayer: "Open my eyes to your truth as I read John 14:27 again."

Write down your thoughts and impressions regarding how this Scripture passage might apply to you:

_____

_____

_____

_____

Review what you gleaned and thank God for these truths.

Yielding Prayer for the Anxious

Let's take some time to pray against worry now.

Shine the Light

Dear Lord,

Please turn on your light of truth over me and my fear and worry. Reveal any areas where I'm focused on my fears and worries more than I'm focused on you.

List the areas the Lord is revealing to you now:

_____

_____

_____

_____

Yield

Put your hand over your stomach and pray the following:

Dear Lord,

I yield all these things as well as my feelings of fear and worry to your peace through your Holy Spirit.

With your hand still on your stomach, take deep breaths and start to relax as you repeat the prayer above until you feel God's peace drop into your spirit.

Forgive

Dear Lord,

I'm not strong enough to let go and forgive myself, you, and those who have caused me distress in any of these areas. Still, I choose to forgive. Therefore, I ask that you, through your Holy Spirit inside me, forgive all. I acknowledge that you, Lord, are without sin. Though you may have allowed these difficulties, you will use them as seeds for miracles. Thank you!

Give It All to God

Dear Lord,

I cast my worries at the foot of the cross. Now they are your worries, not mine. Thank you for setting me free from my worries so I can better trust you.

Pray for Healing

Dear Lord,

Please heal the pain caused by my feelings of fear and worry. Thank you for your supernatural peace.

Exchange the Enemy's Work for God's Peace

Dear Lord,

Please forgive me for giving in to my worries and fears. I close all the doors I have opened to the enemy in this area. In addition, I cancel any plans the enemy has for my life. I also cast out any power or influence from any evil spirits of fear and worry. I pray this in the power of the name and blood of Jesus.

I exchange the enemy's work for God's peace. Send the river of your peace not only to me but also to those who have shared my worries and fears. I pray this also in the power of the name and blood of Jesus.

Praise God—You Are Free!

Thank you, Lord! I'm free!

Pray this prayer whenever you need a redo.

9

Negative

Finding the Secret to a Good Mood

Have this attitude in yourselves which was also
in Christ Jesus.

Philippians 2:5 NASB

It had been a long trip, and after my plane landed at DIA,
I made it through baggage claim and caught the crowded
shuttle to off-airport parking. Once safely in my seat, I took
a deep breath, readying myself for my dive into my purse to
retrieve my keys and a tip for the driver.

But as I searched the dark cavern, shoveling the contents
this way and that, I could not find my keys.

I felt a bead of sweat pop out on my forehead. I was forty
miles from the house, and my husband was off riding his Harley
with his Christian motorcycle friends. He wouldn't be available

to rescue me until late that night. I felt my eyebrows knit together. I was in a pickle.

I looked up from my search to see that for the first time in history my car would be the very first shuttle stop in the parking lot. I shot off a quiet prayer. "What do I do, Lord?"

I felt the peace of his presence. "Trust me," he seemed to whisper.

With the other passengers staring at me, I said, "My keys seem to be missing."

The driver said, "Maybe you left them on the shuttle when you parked. I'll call the office to see if anyone turned them in. What do they look like?"

My cheeks suddenly felt hot. "Uh, the keychain is a plastic square with a book cover on it."

The woman next to me said, "You're an author?"

I gave her a sheepish nod. "What's the title?" the driver asked.

This time I laughed. "Well, it's *When You Don't Know What to Pray*."

"Sounds like you'd better do a little praying now," the woman suggested.

"I'm on it," I said with a grin.

The driver dropped off the other passengers, but I was still fumbling in my purse when the driver drove back to my car. "Maybe we'll be able to see your keys through the window."

Good idea, only they weren't there.

I reboarded the van and kidded with the driver as he drove me to the office so I could do a purse dump and maybe try to call for a ride home.

Once in the office, with the entire contents of my purse piled high on the table, I stared into the deep, black hole of my purse. My keys weren't there, and I shook my purse to prove it. Was that a jingle I heard?

I carefully ran my hand against the interior walls of the purse until I discovered a huge hole in the lining of a zippered pocket. When I pushed my fingers through the hole, I touched my keys!

I happily boarded the van again, and the driver took me back to my car. He said, "You're not like most who lose their keys around here."

"What do you mean?"

"You were laughing and cracking jokes, but my last lady was crying hard."

"Oh no!"

"One man was furious. But it wasn't that he lost his keys; he lost his Lexus. He had me and the manager drive him up and down the rows searching for it for hours. Just before he called the cops, he decided to call home. That's when his wife reminded him he'd driven the station wagon."

So what had made my attitude different from that of the other unfortunate travelers with missing keys and cars? I had called out to God and felt his presence. In that moment, he'd asked me to trust him. I could relax regardless of my difficulty.

I guess you could say that my attitude was both a calling and a choice. We all have the same calling to trust God, and we all can make a choice to stay calm, peaceful even, especially when we know God is with us.

Leadership author John Maxwell writes:

I read a funny story about President Abraham Lincoln that shows the relationship between our choices and their effect upon who we are. An advisor to Abraham Lincoln recommended a particular person for a cabinet position, but Lincoln balked at the suggestion. He said, "I don't like the man's face."

"But sir," said the advisor, "he can't be held responsible for his face."

Lincoln replied, "Every man over forty is responsible for his face."[1]

In other words, what you see in the mirror could very well be a reflection of your attitude, as it says in Proverbs 15:13, "A glad heart makes a happy face; a broken heart crushes the spirit" (NLT).

I know my face often says more about my feelings than I want it to. On days I think I'm secretly feeling sorry for myself, some kindly stranger standing in line at the post office will pat my arm and say, "Cheer up, dear, things will get better." Difficulties beg the question, When our circumstances are difficult, are we doomed to a bad attitude?

Maxwell says, "It's not what happens to you, it's what happens *in* you that counts."[2]

Maxwell's words ring true. You *can* overcome your negative attitude and even replace it with a good mood if you:

- learn to be content
- keep your heart open to the love of God
- take better care of yourself

Learn to Be Content

The apostle Paul talked about contentment in Philippians 4:11–13: "I have learned to be content whatever the circumstances. I know what it is to be in need, and I know what it is to have plenty. I have learned the secret of being content in any and every situation, whether well fed or hungry, whether living in plenty or in want. I can do all this through him who gives me strength."

"I have *learned* to be content." Those were important words to my friend and author Lindsey O'Connor, who as a young wife and mom lived in cramped quarters with her rambunctious brood. Lindsey admits, "I latched onto that phrase. If Paul had learned, then maybe I could too. He didn't say he *was* content in his circumstances; he said he *learned* to be content in them."[3]

And the best part of the passage is that God himself will give us the strength to be content. If you haven't already asked for it, now's the time. Just say, "Give me your strength, Lord, to be content," and he will.

Did someone just sigh because they're wishing I would provide a passage on how to be in control instead of how to be content?

The truth is that God didn't call us to replace him; he called us to trust him. When our negative attitude comes because we don't like where we are or what we have, we need to do a "will" check: God's will versus our will. Take a deep breath and pray along with me:

Dear Lord,

The hard truth is that I'm not in control because if I were things would be a lot different. Did I really just say that to you, Lord? Sorry, I forget sometimes that I am not the Creator but the creation. But I'm your creation. Please be gentle with me and, in your loving way, guide me to where you want to take me. Sometimes I forget that we are on a journey together. And sometimes I have a hard time realizing that the more I fight to have my own way the more you try to teach me the hard lessons of letting go. So in many cases, I've sabotaged myself with stress and unhappiness by clinging to my will instead of reaching for yours. That's why I've decided to say to you, right here, right now, "Your will be done in my life—not mine."

Help me to remember I prayed this so I will trust you along the road ahead, for as I learn to surrender to you, I learn to find contentment in your presence and love. I declare that I trust you to work out everything in my life for the good.

In Jesus's name, amen.

Sometimes we're not in the will of God because we seek the wrong things. A friend of mine told me that she was often on her knees insisting in prayer that God unite her daughter in marriage with a young man she knew from church.

"How do you know he's God's best for your daughter?" I asked her.

"He's perfect! Yet, it's like he doesn't even seem to notice my daughter. I'm going to pray that God will make him marry her."

I soon led my friend in a prayer in which she was able to ask for God's will in the matter. She prayed, "If it be your will, could my daughter marry this young man I've picked out for her? If this man is not your will for my daughter, could you lead her to the man you've picked?"

I'm happy to say that God answered this mother's prayer. No, the daughter did not marry the young man the mother picked out. Instead, the daughter married the man of her dreams, the man God had for her all along, a man who wasn't in the picture when her mother was busy praying for the wrong groom. So you see, asking to be in God's will is a good thing, a thing that can even protect us from a lot of misery because you can't be content if you are not in God's will.

My friend Bill Myers and I recently chatted about our ministry projects. Bill told me, "It's about getting your will aligned with God's will." His remark came just after he'd finished delivering a speech in which he'd shared that his success in both publishing and Hollywood came because a speaker had once challenged him always to say yes to God. That's why he'd left the Midwest as well as his dream of becoming a dentist. That's why he'd moved to Hollywood to make movies.

Though Bill's journey had a few detours, as Bill explained, any frustrations he encountered only caused him to go deeper with God and made him more ready to accomplish the assignments God gave him.

Living in God's will means always saying yes to God. It may not mean you're going to Hollywood, but it may mean you *are* going places you never expected. Just keep in mind that you're not going alone. Jesus is not only guiding this adventure but also sharing it with you.

Keep Your Heart Open to the Love of God

I have a feeling a lot of negative attitudes arise because of love blocks—times we block God's love because we're tired, frustrated, disappointed, or angry. This kind of blockage can lead to soured feelings that can spill onto others. When such an acid spill happens, we are no longer operating in the love of God. It's like 1 Corinthians 13:2 says: "If I had the gift of prophecy, and if I understood all of God's secret plans and possessed all knowledge, and if I had such faith that I could move mountains, but didn't love others, I would be nothing" (NLT).

You don't have to live as if you're nothing because you are something; you are loved by God! Jeremiah 31:3 says, "I have loved you, my people, with an everlasting love. With unfailing love I have drawn you to myself" (NLT).

Stormie Omartian says:

An angry, dour, unforgiving, negative person can get that way for various reasons. He stays that way because of a stubborn will that refuses to receive God's love. The Bible says we have a choice as to what we allow in our heart . . . and whether or not we will harden it to the love of God or not. . . . We choose our attitude. We choose to receive the love of the Lord.[4]

Let's use prayer to open your heart so you can receive and feel more of God's love for you.

Dear Lord,

Sometimes when I am tired, frustrated, disappointed, or angry, I can't feel your love for me. That makes it difficult for me to love others. Please forgive me. When I am tired, remind me to rest so I can be refreshed. When I am frustrated, remind me that despite how things seem you are working in ways that will benefit my life as well as my relationship with you and others. Help me to know that through you everything is going to be all right. When I am disappointed, remind me that I don't have your perspective and that I need to trust you. When I am angry, forgive me for any anger I've directed at you and teach me how to forgive. Remind me how great and wide your love is not only for me but also for those in my life.

If I am treated unkindly, remind me that you've been there too. Remind me that the unkindnesses that have been directed my way are no reflection on your great love for me. Open my eyes to see your love. Open my heart to receive more of it than ever before.

In Jesus's name, amen.

When you feel the warmth of the Father's love, your negative attitude will melt. You'll take to heart the apostle Paul's instruction to "be kind to each other, tenderhearted, forgiving one another, just as God through Christ has forgiven you" (Eph. 4:32 NLT).

When you keep your heart open to the love of God, God's love will flow in abundant supply not only to you but also through you.

Take Better Care of Yourself

It's hard to ward off negative attitudes and bad moods when you don't feel your best. And it's hard to feel your best when your attempts to take care of yourself do anything but help you feel better. For example, if you've ever skipped lunch while sipping a diet soda in an attempt to lose weight, you may have learned that this particular diet plan not only doesn't work but also robs you of energy. If you've ever tried to count getting your heart pumping while sweating through rush hour traffic as aerobic exercise, you may have noticed that this exercise plan doesn't make you fit. And if you've ever tried to catch up on your rest by falling asleep on the couch while watching your favorite show, you may have noticed that those extra winks did little to make you feel refreshed the next morning.

So what does it take to get your body in balance?

It may be time to try a few lifestyle changes, namely, in diet, exercise, and rest. Be sure to talk to your doctor before starting a new program.

To make these changes, you'll need to:

- decide on a few healthy meals to cook, make a list of what you need, and head to the grocery store
- keep a set bedtime with a plan to get at least seven to eight hours of rest each night
- decide on an exercise plan

Exercise, even if you hate jogging? Well, if jogging is out of the question, no sweat. Lysa TerKeurst says:

> Running may not be your thing. So find what is. My Mom loves to say that the best kind of exercise is the kind you'll do. I agree. And while I fully realize my temple may not be God's grandest dwelling, I want to lift up to the Lord whatever willingness I have each day and dedicate my exercise as a gift to Him and a gift to myself. This one act undivides my heart and reminds me of the deeper purposes for moving my body.[5]

I hope you'll take some time to consider these ideas because the better you take care of yourself, the better you'll feel, and the better you feel, the better your mood.

The Story of Peace Continued

Has a bad attitude ever killed someone? The Bible tells of a man with an attitude so terrible that it almost brought death to his entire household.

"Yaakov is here to see you," my maid Urit whispered to me.

I'd been busy setting the table for the feast that my husband and I held for our men during sheep shearing time. Now that the wool of our vast flocks had been sheared and sold to the wool merchants, it was time to celebrate.

But this interruption by our lead shepherd was curious. I set a roasted mutton on the banquet table and turned to Yaakov, who was waiting in the doorway. I wiped my hands on my apron and said, "What is it?"

"We have a problem, Mistress."

"You couldn't go to my husband with it?"

Yaakov shook his head.

"Then tell me quickly," I said, crossing my arms. "The feast is almost ready, and I still have much to do."

The man's brown eyes glistened, and he swiped away a bead of sweat that trickled down his face. "David and his men are on the way to kill us all."

My hand rested on my throat. "For what cause?"

"First, I should tell you that the other shepherds and I often saw David and his men out in the far fields. They were good to us. They protected us from raiders and didn't lay a hand on our flocks."

I nodded. That sounded like the David of the legends, a giant killer who refused to slay an unjust king.

"How noble of David," I said. "So why is he coming to kill us?"

"Just a few moments ago, ten of David's men were with your husband, Nabal, at the tavern, asking him if he would be so kind as to give supplies to David's troops as payment for the work they did to protect our flocks."

"The tavern? So Nabal is already drunk?"

Yaakov only nodded.

"So how much did David's men ask for?"

"Their fee was whatever Nabal felt was fair."

I frowned. "Admirable. How did my husband answer this request?"

Yaakov dropped his eyes. "Nabal said, 'Who does David think he is? In my eyes, he's only a slave on the run from his master, Saul. Should I take my bread and the sheep I've slaughtered for my shearers and give them to a band of outlaws?'"

I felt the blood drain from my face. How could my husband have given such insults to David, not only the leader of a powerful army but also a man who would soon be king? Was my husband so consumed with a purse full of gold that he failed to value his life or the lives of those in his household? Was his attitude so foul that he was too foolish to know when to give honor its due?

I sat down in a chair and stared at the marble floor. "You are right, Yaakov. David's armies will soon arrive with their swords drawn. Our blood will soak into the ground unless . . ."

I looked at the food that my maids and I had placed on the banquet table, then back at Yaakov. "Call the shearers and the shepherds. They must help me and my handmaidens carry this feast to David. If we hurry, we can meet David on the road."

"There could be bloodshed, Mistress Abigail."

"Perhaps, but death is certain if we don't at least try to make amends for the insults of Nabal."

When my servants and I crested the hill not far from town, we almost collided with David and four hundred of his men. David readied his sword to strike, but I placed my basket on the ground and fell facedown into the dirt. I called to the bloodthirsty warrior before me, "Forgive my foolish husband, my lord. Punish me instead. But first, you should know I have brought you a gift and your men provision."

David motioned for silence as I pointed to my frightened servants, all of whom trembled beneath their heavy burdens. "I've brought two hundred loaves of bread, wine, raisins, and roasted mutton, as well as an apology."

David still stared down at me, so I said, "David, you are like a treasure to the Lord. Even though Saul chases you to seek to kill you, you have never done wrong. Because the Lord will fulfill all his promises to you and crown you king of Israel, be careful. Don't commit sin against the Lord. Don't let the slaughter of my clan be a blemish on your record or conscience."

David lowered his sword and reached down to help me stand before him. He said, "Abigail, thank God for your good sense! Bless you for keeping me from murder and from carrying out vengeance with my own hands."

The next morning, when I told the now-sober Nabal what his rank words had almost wrought, he was so shocked that it was as if his heart turned to stone. My husband died ten days later. Some days after that, David asked me to be his wife (based on 1 Sam. 25).

It's clear that Nabal was not the only one with an attitude problem. After hearing Nabal's insults, David was ready to spill the blood of many. It wasn't until Nabal's wife, Abigail, and her servants met David and his men with their fast-food delivery that David calmed down. But it wasn't only Abigail's delivery service that persuaded David to tuck his sword into his belt. Abigail's persuasive words about David's relationship with God also helped.

As his reward for his attitude change, David received the provision of God. In the end, David married Abigail and inherited Nabal's three thousand sheep and his properties.

The lesson is clear. When our attitudes are off the mark with discontent, rage, bitterness, hate, or selfishness, we need to remember God and his love for us. This remembrance will refresh our attitudes and help us honor God and treat others with kindness.

Shine the Light of the Word

What is the secret of improving a negative mood? It can be found in Philippians 2:14–15: "Do everything without complaining and arguing, so that no one can criticize you. Live clean, innocent lives as children of God, shining like bright lights in a world full of crooked and perverse people" (NLT). And Philippians 4:8–9 says, "And now, dear brothers and sisters, one final thing. Fix your thoughts on what is true, and honorable, and right, and pure, and lovely, and admirable. Think about things that are excellent and worthy of praise. Keep putting into practice all you learned and received from me—everything you heard from me and saw me doing. Then the God of peace will be with you" (NLT).

Say this simple prayer: "Open my eyes to your truth as I read Philippians 4:8–9 again."

Write down your thoughts and impressions regarding how this Scripture passage might apply to you:

_____

_____

_____

_____

Review what you gleaned and thank God for these truths.

Yielding Prayer for the Negative

It's time to transform your attitude to the attitude of Christ.

Shine the Light

Dear Lord,
   Please turn on your light of truth over me and my attitude. Reveal to me the attitudes I need to give to you.

List your attitudes about people or situations that the Lord is revealing to you that need improvement:

_____

_____

_____

_____

Yield

Put your hand over your stomach and pray the following:

Dear Lord,
 I yield all my negative attitudes, including the things I've listed, to your peace through your Holy Spirit.

With your hand still on your stomach, take deep breaths and start to relax as you repeat the prayer above until you feel God's peace drop into your spirit.

Forgive

Dear Lord,
 I'm not strong enough to let go and forgive myself, you, and those who have caused me distress in any of these areas. Still, I choose to forgive. Therefore, I ask that you, through your Holy Spirit inside me, forgive all. I acknowledge that you, Lord, are without sin. Though you may have allowed these difficulties, you will use them as seeds for miracles. Thank you!

Give It All to God

Dear Lord,
 I cast my bad attitudes at the foot of the cross. Now my attitudes belong to you. Show me if my diet or lack of sleep is causing my negative feelings and show me how to correct my lifestyle issues. Thank you for setting me free from my negativity and leading me to freedom.

Pray for Healing

Dear Lord,
 Please heal the pain caused by my bad attitudes. Thank you for your supernatural peace.

Exchange the Enemy's Work for God's Peace

Dear Lord,

Please forgive me for giving in to my negative attitudes. I close all the doors I have opened to the enemy in this area. In addition, I cancel any plans the enemy has for my life. I also cast out any power or influence from any evil spirits of lies, trauma, anger, frustration, false expectations, dissatisfaction, and lovelessness. I pray this in the power of the name and blood of Jesus.

I exchange the enemy's work for God's peace. Send the river of your peace not only to me but also to those with whom I've shared my bad attitudes. I pray this also in the power of the name and blood of Jesus.

Praise God—You Are Free!

Thank you, Lord! I'm free!

Pray this prayer whenever you need a redo.

10

Distracted

Finding Your Focus

Our eyes look to the LORD our God.

Psalm 123:2 ESV

It was a sunny December day in New York City. My friend Eva and I were in town to do on-location research for a novel, so we were ready for a day of exploring. I'd come prepared with my huge, blue tote bag, which I'd slung over my shoulder after stuffing it with everything I might need: an umbrella, my coat, snacks, bottles of water, all piled high on top of my wallet.

Eva and I caught the subway from our hotel so that we could walk down Canal Street to take in the sights. We browsed through the faux designer purses and fingered the bright wool scarves and smirked at the fake Rolexes on display. As we strolled, we were caught in a throng of tourists who flowed down the street like a slow-moving river.

As I walked along gawking at the sights around me, a pretty, young woman appeared beside me. She turned to face me, and with her arms opened wide, she side-skipped to my steps as if she were trying to block me from turning right and walking past her. *What in the world is she doing?* I wondered. I craned my neck for a better look, and she seemed to disappear. *Where'd she go?*

Suddenly, I snapped my head to the left, and there she was, her arm rammed deep into my tote bag as her fingers groped for my wallet. I instinctively jerked my tote away from her, and she disappeared into the crowd.

It seemed I'd been preyed upon, unsuccessfully, by a New York City pickpocket. But what struck me about the experience was the pickpocket's maneuver to distract me—to cause me to take my focus away from my tote and to place it in the opposite direction so that she would be free to snatch my wallet.

This business of distraction is the exact strategy the enemy (Satan) uses against us. Distractions, whether constructed by the enemy or produced by our ordinary struggles, can cause us to look in the wrong direction. When this happens, we shift our focus from God to our troubles. Such a shift can cause us to lose our peace, our joy, and our ability to trust in God.

The devotional *Moments of Peace in the Presence of God* explains that distractions can cause us to wonder if God has moved. Yet, as one of the writers says, "God hasn't moved; your focus has—and you must turn your attention back to him. Because he's *still* bigger than your problems and he will certainly help you."[1]

To counteract the distractions that can turn you from God, you need to:

- remember that God can use evil for good
- work through your distractions
- focus on Jesus

Remember That God Can Use Evil for Good

Recently, in one of my quiet times, I heard God's voice in my heart and jotted down these words: "The unseen world is alive and watches you. Your every move is calculated, analyzed, and considered in an effort to create evil schemes against you. But the closer you are to me—the more your focus is on me—the less effective are the plans of the enemy, plans that will evaporate in the presence of my Shekinah glory."

Not sure that the enemy is scheming against you? Then consider that we are in a war. The apostle Paul says in Ephesians 6:12, "For we are not fighting against flesh-and-blood enemies, but against evil rulers and authorities of the unseen world, against mighty powers in this dark world, and against evil spirits in the heavenly places" (NLT).

But even if the enemy means evil toward you, God means it for good. It's like what happened to Joseph, a young man who dreamed God-given dreams of a rosy future in which even his own brothers would bow down to him.

But these dreams of his did little to help him win his brothers' affections; instead, his dreams inspired their intense hostility toward him. Then one fateful day, when Joseph stopped by the far field where his brothers were tending sheep, his siblings decided to kill him. But because none of the young men could actually stomach killing their brother, they decided to sell him as a slave to the first caravan of merchants heading for Egypt.

This was not the rosy future Joseph had anticipated. To make matters worse, he was soon demoted from slave to prisoner on the power of a false charge.

The turnaround came the day a former prisoner of the jail in which Joseph was still incarcerated recommended Joseph to Pharaoh, billing Joseph as the only man in the kingdom who could interpret Pharaoh's dreams. The next thing Joseph knew he was standing before Pharaoh, the most powerful man in the known universe, explaining that Pharaoh's dreams about hungry cows and shriveling stalks of corn signified a coming famine. Pharaoh was struck by Joseph's wisdom and made him not only the head of the famine preparations committee but also his second in command in all of Egypt.

God used the evil deeds committed against Joseph by his brothers to save Joseph's people from famine, for when the famine hit Canaan, Joseph's brothers journeyed to Egypt to buy grain. Joseph had the chance to tell his repentant brothers, "But as for you, you meant evil against me; but God meant it for good, in order to bring it about as it is this day, to save many people alive" (Gen. 50:20 NKJV).

And the best part about this story is that even in the face of so much betrayal and discouragement Joseph kept his eyes on God, always making the best of every situation. Think of how much more Joseph would have suffered if he'd focused on his problems instead of trusting that God would not only transform his troubles but also fulfill the dreams God had put in his heart when he was only a boy.

Charles Stanley explains God's ability to transform the purpose of troubles this way: "But the Father never allows difficulty just for the sake of difficulty—there is always a higher purpose involved. The problem is we cannot always identify

God's higher purpose in the midst of our trials. That's when we must exercise our faith by waiting on His word to us."[2]

Stanley goes on to tell a story about a real estate broker who experienced a seven-year period of financial failure. The broker's thoughts as well as his prayer life became consumed with his finances, and he often wondered why God didn't move to turn his fortune around. Stanley explains that the broker finally realized he had substituted financial security for God. Stanley concludes:

> The Father wanted to be recognized as the Source of all things in my friend's life. As he began renewing his mind spiritually and yielding his rights to the Lord, my friend gained a new freedom in his attitude toward finances. He started a new career and found greater financial blessing than ever before.
>
> God had a great and mighty lesson to teach my friend—a lesson more important than keeping him comfortable. And God kept him uncomfortable until he took his eyes off his circumstances and sought God's mind in the matter.[3]

Stanley's friend had been so distracted by his circumstances that he had failed to seek or focus on God, forgetting that all things work together for good for those who love the Lord (Rom. 8:28).

Does the fact that God can take even the evil plans of the enemy and use them for good mean we should never take a stand against the enemy? Absolutely not. Even Jesus taught us to ask God to "deliver us from the evil one" (Matt. 6:13).

Our comfort is that no matter what happens, or who caused the trouble, we know that through God everything is going to turn out all right. But in the meantime, let's ask for God's deliverance from evil right now:

> *Dear Lord,*
>
> *I am seeking your face, knowing that you are making everything come together for good. The closer I get to you, the more the strategies and purposes of the enemy evaporate in the light of your glory. Thank you, Lord, that I can trust you and that I can ask you to deliver me from evil and into victory. I cancel the evil purposes of the enemy to steal, kill, and destroy and yield to your good purposes of love and life instead—in Jesus's name and through the power of his blood.*
>
> *In Jesus's name, amen.*

Work through Your Distractions

We have to learn how to overcome distractions lest we live our lives as though God isn't involved. The easiest way to recalibrate our focus is through prayer, as explained in 2 Chronicles 7:14: "If my people, who are called by my name, will humble themselves and pray and seek my face and turn from their wicked ways, then will I hear from heaven, and I will forgive their sin and will heal their land."

There are three steps God asks us to take to help us pray so that we can turn our focus back to him and so he can respond to us by forgiving our sin and healing our land. To start this prayer process, we must:

1. Humble ourselves—According to this Scripture passage, we humble ourselves by looking to God for help.

2. Pray—Notice that a list of specific prayers to pray was not provided with this verse. I think this is because God is simply asking us *to* pray.
3. Seek his face—The way you should seek God's face is the same way you would search for a lost child. Desperately!

If you want to push past your distractions so that you can better focus on God, pray the following:

Dear Lord,

I come to you humbly as I look to you for help. For you are the God who wants me to talk to you, to have a personal relationship with you. How amazing that you would want my attention. So I gladly give it to you and say thank you for being who you are, my loving God. I praise your holy name. Lord, I want to know you more, to desperately seek your face. Reveal yourself and guide me! In Jesus's name, amen.

Focus on Jesus

We want to stay focused on Jesus not only because he is powerful but also because he *is* our power. As the psalmist sang in Psalm 16:8, "I keep my eyes always on the LORD. With him at my right hand, I will not be shaken."

If we shift our eyes from Jesus to our difficulties, we are asking for trouble. For example, if we focus on our lack, each bill that arrives in the mailbox will make our heart the poorer. But when we keep our eyes on Jesus as our provider, bill or no bill, we are rich in the confidence that God will provide.

Not only is God our provider, but he also walks on the water of our every storm, just as he did for his bobbing band of followers on the Sea of Galilee. When Peter saw Jesus walking across the storm-tossed lake, Peter called out to him and Jesus answered, "Come!"

But notice that Jesus didn't freeze the water and provide ice skates so Peter could zip on over. Neither did Jesus still the waves so Peter could swim the distance. Jesus didn't even create a moonlit path so Peter could follow it without getting distracted by the lurching waves. With a little intervention from Jesus, Peter could have avoided falling into the drink altogether. So my question is, Wouldn't calming the storm have been more productive than calling Peter to walk across the angry swells in a rain-drenched wind?

The answer to that question is this. Perhaps Jesus chose this turbulent miracle to teach Peter to trust him not in the absence of a storm but through it.

When you focus on Jesus, you will learn to trust him deeply, as Proverbs 3:5–6 instructs: "Trust GOD from the bottom of your heart; don't try to figure out everything on your own. Listen for GOD's voice in everything you do, everywhere you go; he's the one who will keep you on track" (Message).

Let's pray:

Dear Lord,

I want to look at my circumstances through you, with eyes of trust, so that even when you call me to walk through storms I will not go under, but over, as I continue my walk to you. Thank you that you are the one who keeps me on track.

In Jesus's name, amen.

The Story of Peace Continued

Do you think there is a correlation between "meek" and "focused"? Max Lucado believes this is true. "'Blessed are the meek,' Jesus said. The word *meek* does not mean weak. It means *focused*. It is a word used to describe a domesticated stallion. Power under control."[4]

The power of those focused on God comes from God, but it's power under his control—power to overcome, power to defeat enemies. And speaking of meek, how would you like to walk a mile in the shoes of three men who meekly withstood the authority of a king?

When the Babylonians attacked Judea, they killed our king and his sons and took my friends and me captive. We, the sons of Judean nobles, were stripped of our manhood, ensuring we could never father children of our own. We were forced to study the Babylonian religions and ways. Our captors even changed our names as tribute to their sun and moon gods. But my friends and I agreed that though they could change our names they could not change our devotion to Jehovah—the one and only God.

One day King Nebuchadnezzar had a disturbing dream and put his sorcerers to the test, demanding that they not only explain his dream's meaning but also tell him what he had dreamed in the first place. When his sorcerers failed this test, they were put to death. However, our friend Daniel was brave enough to call on God's power to help him know and understand the dream. Nebuchadnezzar was so pleased with Daniel's skill that he promoted Daniel to the governorship of the whole province of Babylon. Daniel then asked the king if his three friends could serve with him.

So that's how we, four Judeans, became rulers over a province that worshiped everything except our wonderful God. But we remained faithful, staying focused on our worship of Jehovah—even when the king built a nine-story-tall golden idol, a giant replica of himself.

Daniel was away on business during the idol's unveiling, leaving myself, Meshach, and Abednego to attend the ceremony. After much fanfare, the king announced that whenever his royal orchestra played his royal song everyone who heard the music had to bow and worship his idol or else be cremated alive in the very smelter that had been used to forge the idol.

My friends and I looked at one another as the harp and other instruments began to play. We watched as the throng around us dropped to the ground to worship the golden image. However, our hearts were so focused on our God that we could not bend even a knee.

Our enemies, who happened to be the officials who were unseated by our sudden rise to power, rushed to tell the king of our disobedience. Nebuchadnezzar was livid and called us to stand before him.

He announced, "How dare my governors not do as I commanded? But I am a patient man. Perhaps you didn't understand the penalty. I will give you another chance to make this right and to bow before my idol. If you do not bow, who will rescue you from my hand?"

I, Shadrach, spoke for the three of us when I said, "Nebuchadnezzar, if we are thrown into the fire, the God we serve is able to save us from your hand. But even if he does not, we want you to know, O King, that we will not serve your gods or worship the object of gold that you have set up."

The king was furious and called for the fiery furnace, already on display for the throng, to be heated seven times hotter. He then called for his strongest soldiers to bind us and drag us to the mouth of the flames. As the soldiers threw us in, they were overcome by the heat and died in agony. But my friends and I did not feel the blaze, only a cool breeze that enveloped us in the heart of the flames. That's when I saw him, his loving eyes, his outstretched arms. My friends and I ran to his embrace.

The voice of the king rose from outside the smelter. "I called for three men to be thrown into this furnace. Why do I see four, one like the Son of God?" Then he called directly to us, "Shadrach, Meshach, and Abednego, servants of the Most High, come out! Come here!"

One by one, we stepped out of the furnace and over the fallen bodies of the soldiers. The king and his people were amazed, for we didn't even smell of smoke. We stood before them without one hair singed and with our clothes unscorched.

The king praised our God for saving us and praised us because we'd withstood his threats. He then forbade anyone else from threatening us because of our faith. But as for me, I will always remember the peace I felt in the furnace, peace I continue to feel as I keep my focus on my God, the one whose very presence can change the atmosphere from death to life (based on Dan. 2–3).

These three friends demonstrated the power of focusing on God. Such a focus helps us to become powerful yet meek as we submit everything to God.

Shine the Light of the Word

Hebrews 12:1–4 encourages us to live a life of focusing on God with these wise words:

> Therefore, since we are surrounded by such a huge crowd of witnesses to the life of faith, let us strip off every weight that slows us down, especially the sin that so easily trips us up. And let us run with endurance the race God has set before us. We do this by keeping our eyes on Jesus, the champion who initiates and perfects our faith. Because of the joy awaiting him, he endured the cross, disregarding its shame. Now he is seated in the place of honor beside God's throne. Think of all the hostility he endured from sinful people; then you won't become weary and give up. After all, you have not yet given your lives in your struggle against sin. (NLT)

Say this simple prayer: "Open my eyes to your truth as I read Hebrews 12:1–4 again."

Write down your thoughts and impressions regarding how this Scripture passage might apply to you:

_____

_____

_____

_____

Review what you gleaned and thank God for these truths.

Yielding Prayer for the Distracted

Lift your eyes unto the Lord and yield your focus to him.

Shine the Light

Dear Lord,

Teach me how to focus on you in every area of my life so I can experience your peace for my soul. Reveal to me the things I let distract me, the things that I focus on more than you.

List the things the Lord is revealing to you now:

_____

_____

_____

_____

Yield

Put your hand over your stomach and pray the following:

Dear Lord,

I yield all these distractions to your peace through your Holy Spirit.

With your hand still on your stomach, take deep breaths and start to relax as you repeat the prayer above until you feel God's peace drop into your spirit.

Forgive

Dear Lord,

I'm not strong enough to let go and forgive myself, you, and those who have caused me distress in any of these areas.

Still, I choose to forgive. Therefore, I ask that you, through your Holy Spirit inside me, forgive all. I acknowledge that you, Lord, are without sin. Though you may have allowed these difficulties, you will use them as seeds for miracles. Thank you!

Give It All to God

Dear Lord,

I cast my distractions at the foot of the cross. Now they belong to you. Thank you for setting me free from my distractions so I can better trust in you.

Pray for Healing

Dear Lord,

Please heal the pain caused by my not staying focused on you. Thank you for your supernatural peace.

Exchange the Enemy's Work for God's Peace

Dear Lord,

Please forgive me for not focusing on you. I close all the doors I have opened to the enemy in this area. In addition, I cancel any plans the enemy has for my life. I also cast out any power or influence from any evil spirits of torment, distraction, worry, and unbelief. I pray this in the power of the name and blood of Jesus.

I exchange the enemy's work for God's peace. Send the river of your peace not only to me but also to those who have shared in my distractions. I pray this also in the power of the name and blood of Jesus.

Praise God—You Are Free!

Thank you, Lord! I'm free!

Pray this prayer whenever you need a redo.

11

Depressed

Finding Real Joy

> The Lord is my strength and my safe cover.
> My heart trusts in Him, and I am helped.
> So my heart is full of joy. I will thank Him
> with my song.
>
> Psalm 28:7 NLV

My daughter Laura has no fingerprints. That's because in order to have fingerprints you must have busy hands. Laura's hands are warm to the touch but have little movement due to her paralysis. Still, her hands are far from useless, as I find that they are perfect for holding. Clasping my fingers around one of Laura's warm hands often brings a smile to her face, a smile I love to receive, a smile I reflect back to her. When I hold her small, misshapen hands, I feel as though I'm holding love itself, a love so pure it brings tears to my eyes. You would think that with all the difficulties my daughter must daily face she would be devastated by her condition. Yet, my daughter never complains. Instead, she sings—happy, wordless songs of praise to a God she knows and loves. She sings out of the joy of her heart.

Thursday afternoons are special because a dear friend, Karis, always stops to give my daughter a fresh coat of colorful nail polish, decorating Laura's nails with swiggles, bright colors, stickers, and designs. Though Laura can't raise her hands to admire her nails, she still loves to have a new coat of polish. She also loves it when we lift her arms, bringing her hands to her face. That's when a little miracle happens—Laura extends her fingers to look at her nails as she giggles in delight.

I'm always amazed by Laura's joy, a joy she gladly shares with all in her life, a joy that comes from a heart close to our heavenly Father. Her heart sings when we play hymns of praise and ushers in the holy presence of God.

How I want to live like that—always in the presence of God, never mind my lack, my frustrations, or my fears because God is near and my trust in him is complete.

In other words, Laura has taught me to strive to be like her, to continually invite God into every area of my life. I love to seek God, to fill my home with songs of praise, and to daily remember that God's love is covering me as I purpose to stay aware of his constant presence.

It's a practice I've not yet perfected. I have good days and bad days, but the more I practice, the sweeter God's presence.

Not only does God want us to practice his presence, but he also wants us to treasure him above all else, even above our abilities, our health, and our bank accounts. Sarah Young's devotional *Dear Jesus* puts it this way: "Many of my children view devotion to me as a duty, and they look elsewhere for their pleasures. They fail to understand that the Joy of My Presence outshines even the most delightful earthly joy."[1]

To find joy in the Lord, we must yield ourselves to his presence. As David sang, "Give me happiness, O Lord, for I give myself to you" (Ps. 86:4 NLT).

Why wouldn't we want to yield to the God who invented joy? Max Lucado says:

> Think about God's joy. What can cloud it? What can quench it? What can kill it? Is God ever in a bad mood because of bad weather? Does God ever get ruffled over long lines or traffic jams? Does God ever refuse to rotate the earth because his feelings are hurt?
>
> No. His is a joy which consequences cannot quench. His is a peace which circumstances cannot steal.
>
> There is a delicious gladness that comes from God. A holy joy. A sacred delight.[2]

Stop wallowing in depression and steep yourself in joy. The best way to accomplish this is to:

- keep God first in your life
- choose joy
- develop an attitude of gratitude

Even if you are clinically depressed, these action steps may give you a boost. But if they don't seem to make a noticeable change, continue to strive to follow these steps, even while you follow your doctor's orders.

Let's bring our quest to understand these concepts to God in prayer:

Dear Lord,

I'm ready to step out of my depression. Teach me how to see you as my treasure and to experience your joy. Help me to keep you first, to seek and choose joy, and to develop an attitude of gratitude. Thank you that the more I give myself to you, the more I feel your joyful presence. I give my difficult emotions to you. Please heal them and teach me how to live in your joy.

In Jesus's name, amen.

Keep God First in Your Life

King David wrote, "Take delight in the LORD, and he will give you the desires of your heart" (Ps. 37:4).

When you let other things compete with your delight in the Lord, you make those things your treasure and therefore your idols. A. W. Tozer once said, "The man who has God for his treasure has all things in One. Many ordinary treasures may be denied him, or if he is allowed to have them, the enjoyment of them will be so tempered that they will never be necessary to his happiness."[3]

The more you have of God, the more your blessings will pale in comparison to the joy you've already found in Christ. You may enjoy your blessings, but you will enjoy the source of your blessings even more.

Don't let depression or the world or its temptations compete with God for the first-place position in your heart. Instead, renew your mind with the Word, worship, and fellowship with other believers while trusting that God will take care of you in every way. As Matthew 6:33 says, "But seek first his kingdom and his righteousness, and all these things will be given to you as well." Let's pray:

> Dear Lord,
>   I give myself to you because you are my treasure. You are the key to my happiness because nothing can compare with you. Give me more of you and your presence so that my joy may be complete.
>   In Jesus's name, amen.

Choose Joy

I often think of how much my daughter, who was disabled at eighteen months of age, has in common with Helen Keller, who when she was eighteen months old suffered from an illness that left her blind and deaf. For five years, Helen lived in a quiet world of darkness in which she was unable to communicate until her teacher, Anne Sullivan, entered her life. It was Anne who turned on the light of understanding in Helen's mind.

Helen had a lot of reasons to be bitter about her condition, but as David Jeremiah says of Helen, "She never pitied herself; she never gave up. She once said, 'The marvelous richness of human experience would lose something of rewarding joy if there were no limitations to overcome. The hilltop hour would not be half so wonderful if there were not dark valleys to traverse.'"[4]

Don't you think that if Helen and Laura can find joy in their circumstances, then perhaps you can also find joy in yours?

Joy is not based on your circumstances but rather on your choice to be joyful. It's just as Max Lucado says in his book *When God Whispers Your Name*: "I choose joy. . . . I will invite my God to be the God of circumstance. I will refuse the temptation to be cynical . . . the tool of the lazy thinker. I will refuse to see people as anything less than human beings, created by God. I will refuse to see any problem as anything less than an opportunity to see God."[5]

When you shift your thinking and begin to see problems as opportunities, you can choose to trust God. You can choose joy.

I can tell you from a recent experience of sitting in a waiting room waiting to hear a doctor's opinion concerning a loved one that instead of waiting in fear and turmoil it's much better to wait with a deep trust in God. It's better to wait knowing that no matter what happens it will create yet another opportunity to see more of God in difficulties.

So instead of sitting in that waiting room swatting away my tears, I put on my headphones and listened to praise music. I felt calm, peaceful, and even joyful in the knowledge that God's presence was with me and that everything was going to be all right.

We are all in the waiting room of life, all waiting to hear opinions, outcomes, revelations, diagnoses, and prognoses. But happily, we do not wait alone. We wait with a God who is already at work in our situations.

So when a problem presents itself, don't go to pieces. Instead, rest in the peace of God as you count it all joy. As James 1:2–4 says, "Dear brothers and sisters, when troubles come your way, consider it an opportunity for great joy. For you know that when your faith is tested, your endurance has a chance to grow. So let it grow, for when your endurance is fully developed, you will be perfect and complete, needing nothing" (NLT).

Let's pray:

> *Dear Lord,*
> *I invite you into my circumstances. Even when my way is filled with pain, I choose to trust in you. I choose joy. Trouble will give me the chance to grow and to endure, and even when I struggle, you are with me. You are my life preserver. In you I trust. Give me your strength to live in joy no matter what.*
> *In Jesus's name, amen.*

Develop an Attitude of Gratitude

Are there days your family wishes you checked your depression or even your bad mood at the door?

"I can't help it," you say. "There are a lot of crazy-making influences in my life beyond my control. Just be glad I've read your book this far and stop meddling with me!"

I too have had both sadness and my inner grump steal my joy, so I really do understand. But what if I suggested that we don't have to live the life of despair? It's time to take our joy back. Let's begin by reading Colossians 4:2: "Pray diligently. Stay alert, with your eyes wide open in gratitude" (Message).

Did it really say gratitude?

Yes, it did. So think of three things you have to be thankful for and write them down.

1. _____
2. _____
3. _____

If you can't think of anything, then I have two words for you: try again. Still can't think of anything? Then try this exercise. Write down your three biggest problems.

1. _____
2. _____
3. _____

Okay, now without delay, thank God for them.

No, I'm not crazy. I'm on a mission to demonstrate a powerful secret that can transform your mood from sad to grateful—and it's all based on 1 Thessalonians 5:18, which reads, "Be thankful in all circumstances, for this is God's will for you who belong to Christ Jesus" (NLT).

How can you be thankful in "all circumstances" when some of the circumstances you're facing are serious or even tragic? How can you be thankful when all you want to know is why? Why did it happen? Why did God allow it?

David Jeremiah writes about a woman whose heart was crushed by a tragedy that happened through no fault of her own. One day she told her pastor, "Your advice to stop asking *why* helped a lot." Then, referring to herself and her husband, she added, "And your sermon yesterday helped to make us able to say, 'We will,' and leave it in God's hands. We will let him use even this, till his plan is perfected."[6]

God miraculously moves in any circumstance we give to his care, and the quickest way to give a circumstance to his care is to thank him for it. If you can learn to stand on this concept, you won't fall. Instead, you'll begin to trust that God is up to good.

Have I tried this exercise myself? Yes, believe it or not, I've actually thanked God for my daughter's situation. Looking back at the first difficult year, as well as the years that have since passed, I can see that our circumstances were full of blessings. Let me take a moment to jot down three of our blessings so you can see them for yourself:

1. Laura is living her divine purpose—to love and to be loved—better than anyone I know.
2. A website that shares her story, www.GodTest.com, has seen over three hundred thousand people come to faith, making my daughter one of the top female evangelists in the country.
3. Her precious spirit has touched the many people she has come in contact with, making a profound difference in their lives.

When I was a brokenhearted mother hovering over her baby in a coma, I would never have dreamed anything good could come out of our predicament. But there came a day I was able to thank God anyway.

When you can live this concept of gratitude, you can live the life my friend and bestselling author Lysa TerKeurst describes:

The reality is that sometimes life is hard. Yet, the Bible says that each day is a gift from God we should rejoice in (Ps.

118:24). Daily adventures with God will add an excitement to your life that will change your whole perspective. No longer is your day just one boring task after another, but rather a string of divine appointments and hidden treasures waiting to be discovered.[7]

So if you haven't already done so, try my experiment and thank God, in an act of trust, for three things you wish were different.

> *Dear Lord,*
> *Paul says in Philippians 2:5, "Have the same attitude that Christ Jesus had" (GW). Help me to find and have this attitude of Christ. Help me also to have gratitude, especially regarding the three problems I am bringing to you now.*

1. _____
2. _____
3. _____

> *As an act of faith, I'm thanking you for these problems because I know you will use them for miracles. Open my eyes to see these miracles and to receive them, even if they are miracles I wouldn't have expected or picked. Thank you, God, that you are in charge and that you are moving in these situations.*
> *In Jesus's name, amen.*

The Story of Peace Continued

Ingratitude is a difficult place to be, a place that Paul and his buddy escaped from, as you'll see in his story below.

I've never known a man to change the way Paul, my friend and fellow Roman citizen, changed after his trip to Damascus. One minute he was caught up in the cause to eradicate all Christians from our Jewish community, and the next minute he'd joined those same Christians in their mission to spread the good news of Jesus Christ. The change was so startling, and his story so compelling, that I too became a believer committed to spreading this good news to others—first with Peter, as I helped him transcribe his letters, and now with Paul in his travels.

Paul and I had journeyed to Philippi to conduct meetings down by the river, telling all who would hear that Jesus is the Messiah. Things were going well until Satan sent a slave girl with a dark gift of fortune-telling to follow us wherever we went. She constantly shouted, "These men are servants of the Most High God, and they have come to tell you how to be saved."

Though her message was true, the enemy was using her to put us in a dangerous situation. Not only was she attracting the wrong kind of attention, but she was also setting herself up as a false believer, a weed in our wheat field. As we were there to build a church that we would soon leave behind, we were worried that she would influence it with Satan's destructive purposes.

Finally, Paul had enough. He turned to the girl and said to the demon within her, "I command you in the name of Jesus Christ to come out of her." Instantly, the demon left.

Her masters had tolerated, even encouraged, her earlier displays toward us, as they'd felt it was a clever way to drum up more customers for their fortune-telling business. But when her powers left her, so did their income and their hospitality toward us. They dragged us into the marketplace before the chief magistrate and charged, "These Jews are throwing our city into confusion!"

At the mention that Paul and I were Jews, the crowd went into a frenzy, calling for us to be beaten. After our brutal beating, we were thrown into prison, and our feet were fastened in painful stocks.

Paul and I sat in the darkness of night, unfed, our raw wounds untended. We weren't alone in this place that smelled of sewage. The prison was filled with other prisoners of the magistrate. Paul and I began to pray aloud, first for our freedom, then for the other men to find freedom in Christ. As Paul prayed, a joy filled my soul. A melody of praise began to rise in my spirit, and I began to sing a psalm of David. "Call out with joy to the Lord, all the earth." Paul's rich baritone voice joined mine. "Be glad as you serve the Lord. Come before Him with songs of joy" (Ps. 100:1–2 NLV).

Suddenly, the ground jerked, twisting our bonds so they broke open. The violent shaking also swung open the doors of our cells. In the raining dust and debris, the jailor stumbled out of his house, just next door. His sword was drawn, and it was apparent he assumed we had already escaped because he pointed the blade at himself. He knew the Romans would torment him before executing him anyway.

But Paul called out, "Stop! We are all here!"

Trembling, the jailor fell on his knees before us. He cried out, "What must I do to be saved?"

I said, "Believe in the Lord Jesus and you will be saved, along with everyone in your household."

Soon the jailor brought us to his home, where he washed our wounds as we joyfully shared the good news of Jesus Christ, news he gladly received (based on Acts 16:16–34).

When we praise, God moves. But more than that, praise causes our hearts to fill with joy when we learn the art of praising God in every circumstance.

Shine the Light of the Word

Paul and Silas were able to find joy in a devastating situation because they chose to praise God in the midst of that situation. Psalm 89:15–18 expresses the result of such a decision:

> Happy are those who hear the joyful call to worship,
> for they will walk in the light of your presence,
> LORD.
> They rejoice all day long in your wonderful
> reputation.
> They exult in your righteousness.
> You are their glorious strength.
> It pleases you to make us strong.
> Yes, our protection comes from the LORD,
> and he, the Holy One of Israel, has given us our
> king. (NLT)

Say this simple prayer: "Open my eyes to your truth as I read Psalm 89:15–18 again."

Write down your thoughts and impressions regarding how this Scripture passage might apply to you:

_____

_____

_____

_____

Review what you gleaned and thank God for these truths.

Yielding Prayer for the Depressed

It's time to yield your depression to God so you can experience the joy he has been waiting to give you.

Shine the Light

Dear Lord,
  Please turn on your light of truth over me and my depression and difficult moods. Reveal any areas of rebellion or depression I need to trade for your joy.

List the areas the Lord is revealing to you now:

_____

_____

_____

_____

Yield

Put your hand over your stomach and pray the following:

Dear Lord,
  I yield all these sorrows, sadness, and depression to your peace and joy through your Holy Spirit.

With your hand still on your stomach, take deep breaths and start to relax as you repeat the prayer above until you feel God's peace drop into your spirit.

Forgive

Dear Lord,

I'm not strong enough to let go and forgive myself, you, and those who have caused me distress in any of these areas. Still, I choose to forgive. Therefore, I ask that you, through your Holy Spirit inside me, forgive all. I acknowledge that you, Lord, are without sin. Though you may have allowed these difficulties, you will use them as seeds for miracles. Thank you!

Give It All to God

Dear Lord,

I cast my sorrows, difficult moods, and depression at the foot of the cross. Now they belong to you. Thank you for setting me free from my sorrows, difficult moods, and depression so I can experience your joy, regardless of my circumstances.

Pray for Healing

Dear Lord,

Please heal the pain caused by my sorrows, difficult moods, and depression. Thank you for your supernatural peace.

Exchange the Enemy's Work for God's Peace

Dear Lord,

Please forgive me for allowing myself to be overcome by sorrows, difficult moods, and depression. I close all the doors I have opened to the enemy in this area. In addition, I cancel any plans the enemy has for my life. I also cast out any power or influence from any evil spirits of sorrow, depression, despair, stress, anger, and unhappiness. I pray this in the power of the name and blood of Jesus.

I exchange the enemy's work for God's peace. Send the river of your peace not only to me but also to those with whom I've shared my despair. I pray this also in the power of the name and blood of Jesus.

Praise God—You Are Free!

Thank you, Lord! I'm free!

Pray this prayer whenever you need a redo.

12

The Peace That Passes Understanding

> Peace I leave with you. My peace I give to you.
> I do not give peace to you as the world gives.
> Do not let your hearts be troubled or afraid.
>
> John 14:27 NLV

When my daughter was in a coma, whenever I tried to rest at night, I'd wake up in a cold sweat with the same question pounding in my heart. *When will it end?* I'd sit up and blink at the darkness and wonder, *How? How will it end?*

Over twenty years have passed, and I still don't know the answers to these questions. However, I rest easier in the knowledge that whatever happens at the end of my paralyzed daughter's life, God will see us through. After all, Laura spent a year in heaven the year she spent in a coma, and I know she'll return to Jesus—who is our final destination.

The first time I asked Laura if she'd seen Jesus while she was "sleeping," she beamed a smile so bright that her face glowed as she lifted her hands above her head in worship. (A pretty good trick for a person who has no purposeful movement.)

As she slowly lowered her hands, I said, "And Mommy believes you sat in Jesus's lap too." Once again, Laura glowed as she lifted her face and flung her hands above her head.

Wow. My daughter *has* been with him, Jesus, the Prince of Peace. Though I can only imagine what her life was like in heaven, I can testify that Laura came back with a peace so deep that it would be hard to believe she hadn't been with the Lord.

Peace. I know you've figured out that peace is the solution to our stress dilemma. Rhonda Rhea says this about peace: "The secret to successfully living in peace is actually no secret at all. A deep, vital relation with the God of peace. Pursue it. Continue to learn about him and grow in your love for him."[1]

Rhea is right. Peace is about going deeper in God. It's about trusting him and yielding our worries and fears to the Holy Spirit—who is already at work inside us. It's about placing our focus heavenward instead of fixing our focus on our struggles. Colossians 3:1–2 advises, "Since you have been raised to new life with Christ, set your sights on the realities of heaven, where Christ sits in the place of honor at God's right hand. Think about the things of heaven, not the things of earth" (NLT).

Even Jesus taught us to pray, "Your kingdom come, your will be done, on earth as it is in heaven" (Matt. 6:10 ESV). Why did Jesus want us to pray like that? Because in heaven there is no death, no fear, no tears, no anxiety, and certainly no stress. So if we pray for God's will to be done on earth as it is in heaven, we'll be blessed indeed.

A lifestyle of peace includes:

- knowing God
- trusting God
- yielding to God
- resting in God's presence

Knowing God

Who is this Jesus we serve? I love how Max Lucado reveals the answer to this question through the many people Jesus came in contact with during his earthly ministry:

"My Lord and my God!" cried Thomas.
"I have seen the Lord," exclaimed Mary Magdalene.
"We have seen his glory," declared John.
"Were not our hearts burning while he talked?" rejoiced the two Emmaus-bound disciples.
But Peter said it best, "We were eyewitnesses of his majesty."
His majesty. The emperor of Judah. The soaring eagle of eternity. The noble admiral of the Kingdom. All the splendor of heaven revealed in a human body. For a period ever so brief, the doors to the throne room were opened and God came near. His Majesty was seen. Heaven touched the earth and as a result, earth can know heaven. In astounding tandem a human body housed divinity. Holiness and earthliness intertwined.[2]

And now, through God's miracle of heaven on earth, God's Holy Spirit has entered our clay temples, once again intertwining holiness and earthliness.

Dear Lord,

I know you are the King of kings and Lord of all. The Holy Spirit has intertwined with my spirit, making me a new creature in you. Not only are you the great and powerful God who created the universe, but you are also the healer of my past, the forgiver of my sins, the comforter who abides in me, and my great and only hope. How can I ever thank you enough? I love you and praise you.

In Jesus's name, amen.

Trusting God

Perhaps you're still having difficulty finding God's peace in your storms. My friend Debbie Alsdorf says:

> If there was never rain, there would not be flowers in the garden of your life. Rain, though soggy and annoying, is a beautiful expression of God's provision. The harsh times in life are the same—though difficult and discouraging, they will prove to be the change agent we need . . . to trust God with everything.[3]

Young Bethany Hamilton learned this lesson despite the fact that heartache was something she never thought she'd experience in the sunny surf of Hawaii. But one day, when she was thirteen, Bethany and her best friend, Alana, lay on their surfboards just off a beach on Kauai's north shore when a fourteen-foot tiger shark silently glided beneath her. As Bethany and Alana waited for the perfect wave, the shark suddenly sank his razor-sharp teeth into Bethany's arm, and the waters around her turned red with her blood.

Though Bethany lost her arm in the attack that day, she did not lose sight of God's will for her life. She overcame her disability by learning to surf competitively again, and she also founded a nonprofit organization called Friends of Bethany that helps other amputees. She even got the chance to play herself in the surfing scenes in the movie *Soul Surfer*, the story of her rise from tragedy.

The loss of her arm made Bethany wise beyond her years, and we can all learn from these words she wrote to teens:

> Maybe you've had something happen in your life you didn't plan on: Your parents divorced or someone you loved died. Maybe you've gotten sick or injured or lost your home to a natural disaster such as a hurricane. Guess what? It's all part of God's plan and he'll use you through it if you are willing. Willingness means letting God's plan become your own, whether it's losing your arm in a shark attack or simply listening to his voice.[4]

God will use whatever happens to you as stepping-stones to his wonderful plan for your life if you are willing to trust him through your pain. Are you willing? If you are, you will see miracles begin to unfold around you, miracles of a nature and magnitude that you might not expect.

Perhaps God is referring to *you* in Jeremiah 29:11: "'For I know the plans I have for you,' says the LORD. 'They are plans for good and not for disaster, to give you a future and a hope'" (NLT).

Dear Lord,

Whom else can I put my trust in but you? For you are the one who makes all things come together not only for the good but also for eternity. Thank you for your plans, even when they include what seems like a disaster. These things are only part of the journey to a wonderful future and hope in you. Thank you!

In Jesus's name, amen.

Yielding to God

Romans 6:13 says, "Neither yield ye your members as instruments of unrighteousness unto sin: but yield yourselves unto God, as those that are alive from the dead, and your members as instruments of righteousness unto God" (KJV).

Billy Graham once explained:

In the original Greek language the words that are translated "yield yourself to God" in the King James Version have a beautiful meaning.

The thought has been translated various other ways by other versions: "Put yourself in God's hands" (Phillips); "Offer yourself to God" (NIV); "Present yourself to God" (New American Standard Version). However the fullest meaning of the word "yield" is to "place yourself at the disposal of someone." In other words, when we yield ourselves to Christ, we do not simply sit back and hope that God will somehow work through us. No, instead we place ourselves at his disposal—we say, in effect, "Lord, I am Yours, to use any way You want to use me. I am at Your disposal, and You may do with me whatever You will. I seek Your will for my life, not my own will." "Put yourself at the disposal of God" (Rom. 6:13 NEB).[5]

We can yield not only our will and our lives to God but also our emotional baggage—our sin, pride, bitterness, worries, anxiety, cares, fleshly desires, and, yes, even our stress. But the beauty of this is that as we yield these emotional toxins to God he trades them for his peace. What a blessing!

Graham reminds us that in this process of yielding "we can hold nothing back,"[6] to which I ask, with the kind of deal God is offering us—peace in exchange for pain—why would we *want* to hold anything back?

Living the yielded life is a process. We have to continually surrender our minds, wills, and emotions to God, because life is not a still photograph. Rather, life is like a movie with plot twists and dark moments and times we say, "I didn't see *that* coming!"

But through it all, God is with us. The more we yield our wills, pain, and turmoil to God, the more we become the new creatures he designed us to be—creatures who though fully human have yielded themselves to him. The truth is that because our spirits are infused with God's Spirit we've become eternal creatures. The life we live now is only temporary. We are only visiting this world while we look forward to the next—our future life in heaven. It's as Jesus explained in John 18:36: "My Kingdom is not an earthly kingdom. If it were, my followers would fight to keep me from being handed over to the Jewish leaders. But my Kingdom is not of this world" (NLT).

Paul said, "Those who use the things of the world should not become attached to them. For this world as we know it will soon pass away" (1 Cor. 7:31 NLT). Our goal then should be to continue the yielding process, living unattached to worldly things but living attached to God and the souls he has given us to love, nurture, work beside, help, and befriend.

It's not always easy to live with the eternal in mind. In the now, we have betrayal, sorrow, pain, and stress. We don't always see a way to live above our heartaches, desires, and longings. Debbie Alsdorf says:

> Truth is, when I am in a meantime place, I often excuse my behavior because I am upset. I suppose that because most people live this way, I have not stopped to realize that God wants so much more from me than living from freak-out to freak-out. I like the idea of living from peace to peace or from glory to glory as I am being conformed to his image one moment at a time.[7]

By continually conforming to God's image, we can break free from our "freak-outs" and live in peace. Galatians 5:22–23 says, "But the fruit that comes from having the Holy Spirit in our lives is: love, joy, peace, not giving up, being kind, being good, having faith, being gentle, and being the boss over our own desires. The Law is not against these things" (NLV).

Dear Lord,

As Billy Graham once advised, I pray that I am yours to use any way you want to use me. I am at your disposal, and you may do with me whatever you will. I seek your will for my life, not my own will.

I know you are making me stronger so that I can endure the race you have set before me, not just so I can stumble

*across the finish line but so I can hear you say these words
to me: "Well done, my good and faithful servant."*

*Give me the will and the strength to continue to yield
everything to you.*

In Jesus's name, amen.

Resting in God's Presence

David Jeremiah says:

> Analysts tell us that at any given moment there are numerous
> wars taking place somewhere in the world. Twenty-four hours
> a day, 365 days a year, people are fighting with each other.
> Those statistics are sad, but here's something that's worse:
> there are other wars taking place that we rarely hear about.
>
> The heart of every human being is a battlefield where
> fear attacks faith, and flesh wars with the spirit; despair
> attacks hope, and hate battles against love. Fortunately for
> us the Bible says that all of those personal battles can be
> won by the Prince of Peace who stands knocking at the
> door of our heart.
>
> Restful hearts are free to face life's battles confidently
> and fearlessly.[8]

Perhaps one of the best benefits of surrendering ourselves to
the Prince of Peace is learning to *live* in his blessing of peace.

In my book *When You Can't Find God*, I tell the story of the
time my four-year-old son collapsed at my feet during a late
night of Christmas shopping. He wrapped his arms around
one of my snow boots, looked up at me, and said, "Mom, I
can't go on. Could you drag me for a while?"

"No," I told him, imagining how dirty he'd get if I dragged him through the shopping mall. "But I can carry you." I leaned down and scooped him into my arms. Then I held him next to my heart as I carried him to the car.[9]

This is exactly what God wants for us. He wants us to yield to him so he can scoop us out of the muck and carry us next to his heart while we rest in his arms.

Rest your weary head on God's chest. Let him do the heavy lifting. Let him carry your burdens. Let him carry you through your trials with his peace. Philippians 4:7 says, "The peace of God is much greater than the human mind can understand. This peace will keep your hearts and minds through Christ Jesus" (NLV).

Dear Lord,
My arms are not only lifted to you in praise but also lifted to you in surrender. I surrender to your presence. Teach me how to rest in your presence and to let you do the heavy lifting. Carry me through my trials in your peace, which is greater than I can understand, a peace that will guard my heart and mind in you.
In Jesus's name, amen.

The Story of Peace Continued

From the moment the angel stood before me and told me not to be afraid, I was filled with questions. I, a virgin, had been chosen to give birth to a son? What would Joseph say, or my parents, or our neighbors?

After all, I was only a teenaged girl whose name meant bitter. My parents were bitter that I had not been born a boy because as a woman it was certain I could not be the Messiah our people so longed for. However, no one had understood that a woman would usher our Messiah into the world.

So I could hardly believe I was gazing up at a beautiful angel who had told me I was highly favored by God and would be the mother of the Son of the Most High.

I could only stammer, "I am the Lord's servant. May it be done to me as you have said."

Shortly after the angel left, I escaped the prying eyes of my village and rushed to see my aunt Elizabeth. Even though I hadn't told her my secret, my aunt said, "Blessed are you among women, and blessed is the child you will bear!"

My situation was harder for Joseph to accept, but the angel appeared to him in a dream and told him that my pregnancy was of the Lord and that my son would save many from their sins.

Though I knew God was with me, many parts of my journey to become the mother of the Messiah were difficult—from hearing the whispers of the town gossips, to the journey to Bethlehem on the back of a donkey, to the birth of my son in a dark cave that served as the innkeeper's stable.

But there were blessings too, like the joy of watching Jesus learn carpentry from Joseph, and his first journey to the temple, where he proved to the scholars that he had a greater understanding of the Word than they did. The one thing I knew about my son was that he was always about his Father's business.

When Jesus put on the mantle of a rabbi and began to walk the countryside with the twelve he called his disciples, I was often in the crowds that gathered to hear him teach. I saw his mighty miracles. The blind could see, the deaf could hear, and the lame could walk. Was there any doubt that my Jesus was the chosen one of God?

I have to admit that when Jesus started his ministry I felt entitled to his attentions. Once his brothers and I stood outside the crowd he was teaching. We had come to Jesus on an important family matter, but instead of stopping his sermon, Jesus gave the crowd the honor of being equal to us, his own family, by saying, "Whoever does my Father's will is the same as my brother, sister, and mother."

His words were hard for me to understand, but harder yet was the ordeal of his arrest the night of the Passover. This is not how I expected things to be!

I stood in the throng at the governor's palace and saw Jesus after the Roman guards had beaten him. I barely recognized him with his precious face so bloody and swollen. He wore a ghastly crown of thorns on his head and stood silently before the mob as they began to cry, "Crucify him!"

My screams of, "Dear Lord, no!" were lost in the death roar surrounding me.

I followed Jesus as the soldiers made him carry his own cross. I fell to my knees weeping as they pounded nails into his hands and feet, then lifted him up on that cross. His body sagged as he struggled to lift himself by his wounded hands and feet every time he needed to take a breath.

My aunt and I held each other as we watched my son slowly die. He looked down at me, and though he was in agony, he said, "Woman, your son," indicating his disciple John. And to John he said, "Here is your mother." John immediately came along beside me and led me away. I leaned heavily on him, especially as we neared the bottom of the hill. Darkness suddenly fell, and the ground beneath our feet shook. Then I heard Jesus's voice call out, "It is finished!"

Jesus was dead. How could this be? The One who came from God to save us from our sins was dead!

Three days later, I was with John and the disciples in the upper room when the women who had gone to bring fresh spices to the tomb pounded on the door. When John opened it, the women poured into the room, crying and laughing at the same time, saying, "He is risen! Jesus is risen from the dead!"

The disciples didn't believe, but I did. I slipped out behind Peter and made my way to the tomb. There I found the stone had been rolled away. Could it be? Hope surged through me. Hadn't Jesus said that the Son of Man had to be put to death before coming back to life three days later?

Late that evening, two of our friends returned from a brief trip to Emmaus to tell us Jesus had appeared to them. Even as they were talking, Jesus suddenly stood before us. My son! Alive from the dead!

His first words? He told us, "Peace be with you."

Jesus had many things still to teach us, many things we still needed to understand. And for the next forty days, we followed him, watching him heal the sick and proclaim that through his death and resurrection he had set us free from our sins.

On that last day, we followed Jesus to a high place that overlooked the city of Jerusalem. While he was still talking, he began to ascend into the sky. We stood with our mouths hanging open as Jesus disappeared until two men, glowing like the sun, suddenly appeared and said, "Why are you standing there looking up at the sky? This Jesus, who was taken from you into heaven, will come back in the same way that you saw him go."

Somehow, I always knew that Jesus would return to God his Father, and the words he had so often said to us rang in my heart. "Peace I leave with you; my peace I give you. I do not give to you as the world gives. Do not let your hearts be troubled and do not be afraid" (John 14:27) (based on the Gospels and Acts 1).

These words of peace that Jesus taught in his earthly ministry are also for you. Your first step in receiving them is to believe that Jesus is the Prince of Peace. Then open your heart to trust him even in times of hardship and trouble.

Shine the Light of the Word

Trusting God is a key to experiencing God's peace, as Isaiah 26:3–4 explains: "You will keep the man in perfect peace whose mind is kept on You, because he trusts in You. Trust in the Lord forever. For the Lord God is a Rock that lasts forever" (NLV). Say this simple prayer: "Lord, open my eyes to see your truth as I read Isaiah 26:3–4 again."

Write down your thoughts and impressions regarding how this Scripture passage might apply to you:

_____

_____

_____

_____

Review what you gleaned and thank God for these truths.

Yielding Prayer for God's Peace

Shine the Light

Dear Lord,

Please turn on your light of truth over me and my stress and fears. Reveal any trust issues that I have toward you or your plan for my life. Reveal to me my self-induced stressors, including a poor diet, a lack of exercise, a lack of fellowship with other believers, and a lack of quiet time and rest.

List the areas the Lord is revealing to you now:

_____

_____

_____

Yield

Put your hand over your stomach and pray the following:

Dear Lord,

I yield all my stress to your peace through your Holy Spirit.

With your hand still on your stomach, take deep breaths and start to relax as you repeat the prayer above until you feel God's peace drop into your spirit.

Forgive

Dear Lord,

I'm not strong enough to let go and forgive myself, you, and those who have caused me distress in any of these areas.

Still, I choose to forgive. Therefore, I ask that you, through your Holy Spirit inside me, forgive all. I acknowledge that you, Lord, are without sin. Though you may have allowed these difficulties, you will use them as seeds for miracles. Thank you!

Give It All to God

Dear Lord,

I cast my fears and stress at the foot of the cross. Now they belong to you. Thank you for setting me free from my stress so I can live in your peace that passes understanding.

Pray for Healing

Dear Lord,

Please heal the pain caused by my stress. Thank you for your supernatural peace.

Exchange the Enemy's Work for God's Peace

Dear Lord,

Please forgive me for allowing myself to be overcome by stress. I close all the doors I have opened to the enemy in this area. In addition, I cancel any plans the enemy has for my life. I also cast out any power or influence from any evil spirits of lies who say your peace isn't for me, in the power of the name and blood of Jesus.

I exchange the enemy's work for God's peace. Send the river of your peace not only to me but also to those who *have shared my stress. I pray this also in the power of the name and blood of Jesus.*

Praise God—You Are Free!

Thank you, Lord! I'm free!

Pray this prayer whenever you need a redo.

Conclusion

Finding God's Peace

Thank you so much for traveling with me on this journey to leave our stress behind as we go deeper into the peace of God. What a journey it has been. We've learned to yield our feelings of being overwhelmed, stuck, frustrated, burdened, hopeless, offended, anxious, negative, distracted, and depressed to Jesus, the Prince of Peace, by the power of the Holy Spirit.

This skill of yielding to the peace of God is a skill you've practiced as you read through the pages of this book. It's also a skill you can continue to master throughout your walk with God.

So now, at the first signs of stress, take a deep breath and begin to yield your burdens to the Lord as you also yield to his peace. As Jesus told his disciples, "Peace be with you" (Luke 24:36).

Now enjoy and practice God's peace no matter what your circumstances.

God bless you.

Notes

Introduction: The Problem of Stress

1. www.psychologytoday.com/blog/the-race-good-health/201212/4-healthy-ways-cope-stress.

2. Ibid.

3. www.webmd.com/balance/stress-management/stress-management-topic-overview.

4. http://en.wikipedia.org/wiki/Stress_(biology).

5. http://dictionary.reference.com/browse/stress?s=t.

Chapter 1: The Key to Peace

1. Max Lucado, *A Gentle Thunder: Hearing God through the Storm* (Nashville: Thomas Nelson, 1995), 68.

2. Ibid., 70.

3. Billy Graham, *The Holy Spirit: Activating God's Power in Your Life* (Grand Rapids: Zondervan, 1978), 113.

Chapter 2: Overwhelmed

1. http://dictionary.reference.com/browse/overwhelm?s=t.

2. Sarah Young, *Jesus Calling: Enjoying Peace in His Presence* (Nashville: Thomas Nelson, 2004), May 10.

Chapter 3: Stuck

1. Phillip Keller, *A Shepherd Looks at Psalm 23* (New York: Harper-Collins, 1970), 54–55.

2. Sarah Young, *Dear Jesus* (Nashville: Thomas Nelson, 2007), 121.

3. *Nature, International Weekly Journal of Science*, January 4, 2012, "Demonstration of Temporal Cloaking," http://www.nature.com/nature/journal/v481/n7379/full/nature10695.html#/contrib-auth.

4. Katie Drummond, "Pentagon Scientists Create Time Hole to Make Events Disappear," January 4, 2012, http://www.wired.com/dangerroom/2012/01/time-hole/#more-68739.

Chapter 4: Frustrated

1. Max Lucado, *Life to the Max* (Nashville: Thomas Nelson, 2011), http://tinyurl.com/akjxw24.

2. Ibid.

3. Billy Graham, *Dealing with Doubt: A Thomas Nelson Study Series Based on The Journey by Billy Graham* (Nashville: Thomas Nelson, 2007), 4.

4. Ibid.

5. Stormie Omartian, *Just Enough Light for the Step I'm On: Trusting God in the Tough Times* (Eugene, OR: Harvest House, 1999), 41–43.

6. Ibid.

Chapter 5: Burdened

1. Janet Holm McHenry, *Daily Prayer Walk* (Colorado Springs: Water-Brook, 2002), 175.

Chapter 6: Hopeless

1. Charles Stanley, *Handle with Prayer: Unwrap the Source of God's Strength for Living* (Colorado Springs: David C. Cook, 1982), 11.

2. Max Lucado, *You'll Get through This—Hope and Help for Your Turbulent Times* (Nashville: Thomas Nelson, 2013), 201.

Chapter 7: Offended

1. Pam Farrel, *Fantastic after Forty* (Eugene, OR: Harvest House, 2007), 172.

2. Dr. Bill Bright, *The Joy of Supernatural Thinking* (Colorado Springs: Victor, 2005), 80–81.

3. Karol Ladd, *Thrive, Don't Simply Survive: Passionately Live the Life You Didn't Plan* (New York: Simon & Schuster, 2009), 109.

Chapter 8: Anxious

1. http://pediatrics.about.com/cs/safetyfirstaid/a/snake_bites.htm.

2. Max Lucado, *Fearless: Imagine Your Life without Fear* (Nashville: Thomas Nelson, 2009), 10.

3. Neil T. Anderson and Rich Miller, *Freedom from Fear* (Eugene, OR: Harvest House, 1999), 25.

4. Sarah Young, *Jesus Calling: Enjoying Peace in His Presence* (Nashville: Thomas Nelson, 2004), May 19.

5. Sue Falcone, *Lighthouse of Hope: A Day by Day Journey to Fear Free Living* (Kindle Edition) (Lighthouse Publishing of the Carolinas), May 11, 2012.

6. Sarah Young, *Dear Jesus* (Nashville: Thomas Nelson, 2007), 106.

Chapter 9: Negative

1. John Maxwell, *Your Road Map for Success: You Can Get There from Here* (Nashville: Thomas Nelson, 2002), 51.

2. Ibid.

3. Lindsey O'Connor, *If Mama Ain't Happy, Ain't Nobody Happy!* (Eugene, OR: Harvest House, 1996), 102.

4. Stormie Omartian, *The Power of a Praying Wife* (Eugene, OR: Harvest House, 1997), 150.

5. Lysa TerKeurst, *Made to Crave: Satisfying Your Deepest Desire with God, Not Food* (Grand Rapids: Zondervan, 2010), 94.

Chapter 10: Distracted

1. Lila Empson, ed., *Moments of Peace in the Presence of God: Morning and Evening Edition* (Bloomington, MN: Bethany, 2004), 657.

2. Charles Stanley, *Handle with Prayer: Unwrap the Source of God's Strength for Living* (Colorado Springs: David C. Cook, 1982), 10.

3. Ibid.

4. Max Lucado, *Grace for the Moment—Women's Edition: Inspirational Thoughts for Each Day* (Nashville: Thomas Nelson, 2007), 263.

Chapter 11: Depressed

1. Sarah Young, *Dear Jesus* (Nashville: Thomas Nelson, 2007), 96.

2. Max Lucado, *The Applause of Heaven* (Nashville: Thomas Nelson, 1990), 13.

3. A. W. Tozer, *The Pursuit of God* (Rockville, MD: Serenity Publishers, 2009), 20.

4. David Jeremiah, *Turning toward Joy* (Colorado Springs: David C. Cook, 2006), 40.

5. Max Lucado, *When God Whispers Your Name* (Nashville: Thomas Nelson, 1994), 71–72.

6. Jeremiah, *Turning toward Joy*, 42.

7. Lysa TerKeurst, *What Happens When Young Women Say Yes to God* (Eugene, OR: Harvest House, 2014), 166.

Chapter 12: The Peace That Passes Understanding

1. Rhonda Rhea, *Whatsoever Things Are Lovely* (Grand Rapids: Revell, 2009), 218.

2. Max Lucado, *God Came Near* (Nashville: Thomas Nelson, 1986), xv.

3. Debbie Alsdorf, *A Woman Who Trusts God: Finding the Peace You Long For* (Grand Rapids: Revell, 2011), 14.

4. Bethany Hamilton, *Soul Surfer Devotionals* (Nashville: Thomas Nelson, 2006), 1.

5. Billy Graham, *The Holy Spirit* (Grand Rapids: Zondervan, 1978), 119.

6. Ibid.

7. Alsdorf, *A Woman Who Trusts God*, 19.

8. David Jeremiah, *1 Minute a Day* (Nashville: Thomas Nelson, 2008), 123.

9. Linda Evans Shepherd, *When You Can't Find God: How to Ignite the Power of His Presence* (Grand Rapids: Revell, 2011), 167.

Linda Evans Shepherd is the author of over thirty books, including *When You Don't Know What to Pray: How to Talk to God about Anything* and *When You Can't Find God: How to Ignite the Power of His Presence*, and the co-author of the popular series the Potluck Club and the Potluck Catering Club. Linda is an international speaker and media personality, is the creator of RightToTheHeart.tv, and appears as a frequent host of Daystar's Denver Celebration.

She's the leader of the Advanced Writers and Speakers Association and the president of the nonprofit ministry Right to the Heart, which has seen over 500,000 people come to faith. She's married and has two children. For more, visit www.sheppro.com.